Religion and Belief in United Kingdom Employment Law

Law and Religion

Volumes published in this Brill Research Perspectives title are listed at *brill.com/rplr*

Religion and Belief in United Kingdom Employment Law

An Introduction to the Case-Law

By

Frank Cranmer

BRILL

LEIDEN | BOSTON

This paperback book edition is simultaneously published as issue 1.3 (2017) of *Law and Region*,
DOI 10.1163/24682993-12340003.

Library of Congress Control Number: 2017957921

Typeface for the Latin, Greek, and Cyrillic scripts: "Brill". See and download: brill.com/brill-typeface.

ISBN 978-90-04-36157-7 (paperback)
E-ISBN 978-90-04-36164-5 (e-book)

Published by Koninklijke Brill NV, Leiden, The Netherlands.
Koninklijke Brill NV incorporates the imprints Brill, Brill Hes & De Graaf, Brill Nijhoff, Brill Rodopi, Brill Sense and Hotei Publishing.

This book is printed on acid-free paper and produced in a sustainable manner.

Religion and Belief in United Kingdom Employment Law

An Introduction to the Case-Law

By

Frank Cranmer

BRILL

LEIDEN | BOSTON

This paperback book edition is simultaneously published as issue 1.3 (2017) of *Law and Region*, DOI 10.1163/24682993-12340003.

Library of Congress Control Number: 2017957921

Typeface for the Latin, Greek, and Cyrillic scripts: "Brill". See and download: brill.com/brill-typeface.

ISBN 978-90-04-36157-7 (paperback)
E-ISBN 978-90-04-36164-5 (e-book)

Published by Koninklijke Brill NV, Leiden, The Netherlands.
Koninklijke Brill NV incorporates the imprints Brill, Brill Hes & De Graaf, Brill Nijhoff, Brill Rodopi, Brill Sense and Hotei Publishing.

This book is printed on acid-free paper and produced in a sustainable manner.

Contents

Preface and Acknowledgements

The bare bones beneath what follows is a paper that I first prepared about five years ago for the Churches' Legislation Advisory Service (CLAS) at the request of the then General Secretary of the United Reformed Church, the Revd Roberta Rominger. The original intention was merely to provide a simple and concise list of case-notes on clergy employment—intended for church administrators rather than for lawyers—against the inevitable day when some aggrieved cleric would sue his or her denomination for wrongful or unfair dismissal. In the course of successive revisions, however, the text grow'd like Topsy, partly because of the accretion of further clergy employment cases and partly because it slowly dawned on me that the wider issues of religion in employment were of almost as much interest and relevance to some denominations as the narrower one of the terms and conditions of clergy tenure.

So I should like to thank Roberta for her original suggestion: had it not been for her, this would never have been written. But I am not a specialist employment lawyer; and even more important has been the extremely generous help I have received from John Duddington, editor of *Law & Justice*, and from Maria Strauss, Rachel Lewis and Sam Talbot Rice of Farrer & Co. Sam, Maria and John, in particular, crawled over my text with a fine-tooth comb for errors of law and doubtful conclusions—but any remaining infelicities, misjudgements or downright howlers are entirely my responsibility, not theirs.

The law is that in force on 1 September 2017. Wherever possible, I have used neutral citations from BAILII.

Frank Cranmer
Skye, September 2017

Religion and Belief in United Kingdom Employment Law: An Introduction to the Case-Law

Frank Cranmer
Fellow, St Chad's College, Durham, Honorary Research Fellow
Centre for Law & Religion, Cardiff University
frank.cranmer@centrallobby.com

Abstract

The interactions between religious belief and employment law touch on a wide variety of issues, ranging from basic questions about the definitions of 'religion' and 'belief'—and, indeed, of 'employment'—to issues such as time off for religious observance, religious dress in the workplace and the extent to which an employer can impose its religious values on its workforce. This monograph looks at the major issues of religion in relation to employment law in the United Kingdom, primarily by reference to the recent case-law.

Keywords

law – religion and belief – employment – Article 9 ECHR

Introduction

Why 'Religion and Belief' in Employment Law?

'Employment Law is Characterised by a Relatively High Level of Complexity and Technicality'

So said Lord Hughes JSC in a recent case in which the Supreme Court quashed the Employment Tribunals and the Employment Appeal Tribunal Fees Order 2013.[1] And if employment law generally is 'characterised by a relatively high

1 *R (UNISON) v Lord Chancellor* [2017] UKSC 51 at [28]. The Order had imposed fees for bringing tribunal claims in employment cases; prior to the commencement of that Order, no fee had been payable.

 | DOI 10.1163/9789004361645_002

level of complexity and technicality', to apply that description to employment law as it relates to the manifestation of religion or belief would be a major understatement. The interactions between employment law and religious belief touch on a wide variety of issues, ranging from the basic question, 'exactly what constitutes a "religion" or "belief"?' to 'what kinds of religious dress do my employees have a right to wear to work?', 'can my employee demand time off work for a religious festival?' and 'what religious standards—if any—can I, as an employer, demand of my employees?'. My purpose, therefore, is to provide an overview of some of the current issues and problems surrounding the law relating to employment by religious organisations and the manifestation of religion in the workplace, primarily by examining recent case-law.

I begin by setting out the institutional, demographic and legislative context against which issues of religion and employment are played out. Next, I look at the issue of employment status and discrimination, starting with the basic terminology. I then consider the employment position of ministers of religion generally, but with separate discussions of the position of clergy in the Church of England—which, as we shall see, is very much a special case—and, to a more limited extent, in the Church of Scotland. Next, I turn to the position of lay employees, volunteers and the rather vexed question of the status of interns. The next major issue is the religious exception in employment, the definition of 'philosophical belief', the 'Genuine Occupational Requirement' and the right of laypeople to manifest their religion in secular employment. I then discuss some of the recent cases on vicarious liability, especially in relation to historic sexual abuse. Finally, I conclude with some general observations on possible future developments in the law.

I should emphasise that what follows is emphatically *not* a formal, technical treatise on the religious aspects of employment law. It aims to be exactly what it says on the tin—an introduction and no more than that—and it concentrates almost entirely on the decided cases rather than on the academic commentary surrounding them. Furthermore, just over three-quarters of the cases cited have been decided within the last ten years.

For that, I make no apology. Disputes about religious manifestation have become more and more common as people have become ever readier to assert their rights, both under domestic legislation and the ECHR, while employment cases, perhaps more than in any other area of private law, tend as often as not to turn on the facts—which is a further reason for their complexity and a mantra that will keep recurring in what follows.

The Institutional Context

For those unfamiliar with the institutional and religious landscape of the United Kingdom it may be helpful to begin with a very brief outline of the context for the subsequent discussion.

The United Kingdom consists of three legal jurisdictions—England and Wales, Scotland and Northern Ireland—with four legislatures. Legislative devolution since the mid-1990s has resulted in an asymmetrical distribution of powers from the United Kingdom Parliament to the Northern Ireland Assembly, the Scottish Parliament and the National Assembly of Wales, each of which has a different legislative competence. England, Northern Ireland, Scotland and Wales also differ in relation to the legal status of the religious organisations within them.

England

The Church of England is the Church 'established by law' in England; and Measures and secondary legislation of the Church's General Synod are part of the general law of England. Once approved by an affirmative resolution of each House of Parliament, a Measure is given Royal Assent in the same way as a secular statute and is published as part of the bound volumes of the annual Statute Book. New or amending Canons of the Church of England, which also form part of English ecclesiastical law, are likewise given Royal Assent before being promulged but, unlike Measures, they are not subject to approval by Parliament.

The courts of the Church of England are part of the general system of courts, the senior ecclesiastical judge—the Dean of the Arches Court of Canterbury and Auditor of the Chancery Court of York[2]—is appointed by the Crown (Moore, 1992: 7–8) and the decisions of the ecclesiastical courts are subject to judicial review by the High Court on the same basis as those of secular courts and tribunals (Doe, 1996: 149).

Scotland

Unlike the Church of England, the Church of Scotland belongs to the Reformed tradition and its ecclesiology is Presbyterian. Article III of the Articles Declaratory annexed to the Church of Scotland Act 1921 declares it to be 'a national Church representative of the Christian Faith of the Scottish people'; and whether that amounts to 'establishment' is a matter on which opinions differ.

---

2 Separate offices but held by the same person.

Brown *et al.* (2016: 71) conclude that 'the Church of Scotland Act 1921 does not betoken establishment' and suggest the Act should be understood in terms of the Scots law of trusts and in the context of the reunion negotiations between the Church of Scotland and the United Free Church which bore fruit in 1929. The Church still enjoys 'unique recognition by the Crown' (Brown *et al.*, 2016: 75) and there remain some 'lingering aspects' of the statutory recognition of its courts (Brown *et al.*, 2016: 85); but 'establishment' as a label no longer has any great significance in the Scottish context and for all practical purposes has become a non-issue.[3]

In the Inner House of the Court of Session in *Percy*,[4] Lord President Rodger described the status of the Church's law like this:

> despite their outward appearance, *the laws of the Church operate only within the Church and her courts adjudicate only on matters spiritual.* In other words, the formality and indeed solemnity of all these transactions and proceedings does not disclose an intention to create relationships under the civil law, rather, it reflects the serious way in which the Church regulates the matters falling within the spiritual sphere [14: emphasis added].

So the Church of Scotland still remains in some sense qualitatively different from any other religious community in Scotland—but its law does not have the same status or reach in Scots law as the law of the Church of England has in English law.

Northern Ireland and Wales

There is no establishment of religion in Northern Ireland or Wales. Long before Partition, the Irish Church Act 1869 disestablished the Church of Ireland in both parts of the island. With the exception of a handful of border parishes, the territory of the Welsh dioceses of the Church of England was disestablished as from March 1920 under the terms of the Welsh Church Act 1914 and became the Church in Wales—the process of disestablishment having been

3 Though that was not always the case. In *General Assembly of the Free Church of Scotland v Lord Overtoun: Macalister v Young* [1904] AC 515, 1904 7 F (HL) 1, a minority of the Free Church averred—successfully—that by uniting with the United Presbyterians the majority had betrayed the *Westminster Confession of Faith* generally, repudiated the 'Establishment Principle' and departed from the specific terms of the *Confession* as set out in Chapter XXIII: *Of the Civil Magistrate*. For a recent discussion of the case see Lyall (2016: 123–128).

4 *Percy v Board of National Mission of the Church* [2001] ScotCS CSIH 65.

interrupted by the Great War. Moreover, s.3 (1) of the Welsh Church Act declares that:

> As from the date of disestablishment ecclesiastical courts and persons in Wales and Monmouthshire shall cease to exercise any jurisdiction, and the ecclesiastical law of the Church in Wales shall cease to exist as law.[5]

Nevertheless, the Church in Wales retains a very few 'hangover' features from its former established status, most notably the common law right of parishioners to marry in the parish church, whether members of the Church or not.[6]

The Religious Demography of the UK

According to 2015 estimates, the United Kingdom's population was slightly over 65 million (Office for National Statistics, 2016), of which approximately 59 per cent was Christian in England and Wales, 54 per cent in Scotland and 82.5 per cent in Northern Ireland. There are no separate figures for England and Wales, but in 2016 it was estimated that 15 per cent of the population of Great Britain identified themselves as Anglicans[7] and 9 per cent as Roman Catholics, while 53 per cent had no religion at all (NatCen, 2017). The two largest Scottish denominations are the Church of Scotland, with a claimed adherence of 32 per cent of the population, and the Roman Catholic Church with 16 per cent. Census figures for Northern Ireland indicate that 41 per cent of the Christian population is Roman Catholic and 41.5 per cent Protestant—mainly Presbyterians or adherents of the Church of Ireland.

The headline figures from the 2011 Census (Office for National Statistics, 2014) suggested that the Muslim community made up 4.8 per cent of the population of England and Wales and 1.4 per cent in Scotland. Other religious groups—Hindus, Sikhs, Jews and Buddhists—each made up less than 2 per cent of the population of England and Wales and a combined 0.8 per cent in Scotland, while in Northern Ireland, non-Christian religious groups represented less than 1 per cent. But we are now past the mid-point between censuses; and the suspicion is that the some of the non-Christian faith communities have grown in size since 2011, not least because of their relatively lower age-profiles.

5 S.21 Irish Church Act 1869—on which the Welsh provision was based—made similar provision for the abolition of ecclesiastical law in Ireland 'except in so far as relates to matrimonial causes and matters'.

6 See Watkin (1990) and Cranmer (2015).

7 Of whom the vast majority will be in England and Wales, because the (Anglican) Scottish Episcopal Church has rather fewer than 100,000 adherents in a population of over five million.

So the framework within which issues of employment and religious belief are played out is increasingly complex. Paradoxically, the United Kingdom—especially England—is becoming increasingly multi-faith while at the same time becoming increasingly secular. It continues to give special constitutional recognition to a particular Christian community—the Church of England—under a very distinct legal status but is nevertheless firmly committed to equal treatment for citizens of all faiths and none. In the circumstances, it is hardly surprising that conflicts and tensions sometimes arise.

The Legislative Context

To put it at its most basic, 'employment' is a situation that arises from a mutuality of obligations under which A, 'the employer', provides work for B, the 'employee' or 'worker', and controls how, when and where that work is done. In return, B performs the work in person and is paid for it. However, the rights and obligations of employers and those who work for them are regulated not just by the law of contract/obligations but by a complex series of legislative provisions and judicial decisions.

England, Scotland and Wales

In Great Britain, employment law is a matter reserved to the Westminster Parliament.[8] The primary legislative provision in Great Britain relating to employment issues generally is the Employment Rights Act 1996, which sets out employment rights generally and makes no specific mention of religion.

The Working Time Regulations 1998, which apply to Great Britain only, include 'workers officiating at religious ceremonies in churches and religious communities' as workers likely to fall within the category of those excluded from the provisions on maximum weekly working time, length of night work, daily and weekly rest periods and rest breaks, on the grounds that such a person is a worker where, on account of the specific characteristics of the activity in which he is engaged, the duration of his working time is not measured or predetermined or can be determined by the worker himself.[9]

---

8 As to Scotland, see Scotland Act 1998 Schedule 5 Head H. The Government of Wales Acts 1998 and 2006 did not confer legislative competence on the National Assembly for Wales in respect of employment law and the Wales Act 2017 maintains that position: Schedule 7A inserted into the Government of Wales Act 2006 by the 2017 Act includes 'Head H–Employment' in the matters reserved to Westminster.

9 Regulation 20(c). A worker 'officiating at religious ceremonies in churches etc.' does not a *necessarily* fall within the exemption. A job title does not *of itself* trigger the exemption; rather, the Regulations suggest that such workers are likely to have 'unmeasured working time' and therefore be subject to the exemption.

The Employment Equality (Religion or Belief) Regulations 2003 made specific provision in relation to discrimination on grounds of religion or belief, discrimination by way of victimisation, harassment on grounds of religion or belief and discrimination in employment and vocational training. The Equality Act 2010 subsumed the content of the 2003 Regulations, which it revoked; and much of the subsequent discussion refers to its provisions.

Northern Ireland

Neither the Employment Rights Act 1996[10] nor the Equality Act 2010 extends to Northern Ireland. Both employment and equality law are matters devolved to the Northern Ireland Assembly, though during direct rule,[11] when the Westminster Parliament legislated directly for the Province by statutory instrument, it was the policy of the United Kingdom Government that most statutory employment rights and obligations in Northern Ireland should be aligned with those in Great Britain. The equivalent Northern Ireland legislation, therefore, is the Employment Rights (Northern Ireland) Order 1996—as amended in order to implement Council Directive 2000/78/EC establishing a general framework for equal treatment in employment and occupation ('the Framework Directive')—and the Fair Employment and Treatment (Northern Ireland) Order 1998, as amended,[12] which defines 'discrimination' as

(a) discrimination on the ground of religious belief or political opinion; or

(b) discrimination by way of victimisation.[13]

---

10 With the exceptions of ss.201, 236, 238 and 243–245.

11 Which ended in 1999 after the conclusion of the Belfast Agreement in 1998, when employment law once again became a matter devolved to the Northern Ireland Assembly and Executive. At the time of writing, the future of devolved government in Northern Ireland was unclear.

12 For a recent discussion of the law relating to the employment of ministers of religion in Northern Ireland, see Barry Forde (2017), who points out that the Employment Rights (NI) Order defines a worker as someone who 'undertakes to do or perform personally any work or services for another party' but that, in anti-discrimination legislation and legislation to comply with the Working Time Directive, 'employee' is defined in wider terms more akin to that of 'worker'. Though particular types of employment and office holding are addressed, 'ministers of religion' are never expressly mentioned. Moreover, 'any employment or occupation as a clergyman or minister of a religious denomination' is specifically exempted from the provisions of the Fair Employment and Treatment (NI) Order by paragraph 70(1)(a): *Excepted employments, etc.*

13 Paragraph 3(1): *"Discrimination" and "unlawful discrimination".*

Employment issues generally are heard by Industrial Tribunals; complaints of discrimination on the grounds of religious belief or political opinion are heard by the Fair Employment Tribunal. *The discussion that follows is primarily concerned with the law in Great Britain and only passing reference will be made to the law in Northern Ireland.*[14]

The Statutory Framework

Equal Treatment, Discrimination, Harassment and Victimisation

Discrimination, whether direct or indirect, harassment and victimisation are 'prohibited conduct' under the Equality Act 2010.[15]

Direct and Indirect Discrimination

Under the 2010 Act, the basic principle of equal treatment is that it is unlawful to discriminate *directly* against someone with a 'protected characteristic'—enumerated as: disability, gender reassignment, marriage and civil partnership, pregnancy and maternity, race, religion or belief, sex, and sexual orientation[16]—or to discriminate *indirectly* without justification. S.10 (Religion or belief) defines 'religion' as 'any religion and a reference to religion includes a reference to a lack of religion' and 'belief' as 'any religious or philosophical belief and a reference to belief includes a reference to a lack of belief'. Furthermore:

(3) In relation to the protected characteristic of religion or belief—
   (a) a reference to a person who has a particular protected characteristic is a reference to a person of a particular religion or belief;
   (b) a reference to persons who share a protected characteristic is a reference to persons who are of the same religion or belief.

Under the 2010 Act, *direct* discrimination occurs where a person (A)—in this context, an employer—treats a person (B) who has a protected characteristic less favourably than others are treated (or would be treated) because of that characteristic.[17] One of the protected characteristics is religion or belief so, for

14 For further details on Northern Ireland, see Paul Gillen and Brian Morgan (2013).

15 See Chapter 2 of the Act.

16 S.4 Equality Act 2010: there is no corresponding consolidated legislation for Northern Ireland, where equality issues are dealt with piecemeal by a range of statutory instruments.

17 S.13(1).

example, it would be directly discriminatory for an employer refuse to employ a Hindu who had all the necessary skills and competences for a vacant post *merely because he or she was a Hindu*, on the assumption that a non-Christian would not fit in socially with a predominantly Christian workforce.[18]

Indirect discrimination is more subtle: it occurs where A applies a 'provision, criterion or practice' (PCP) to B which is discriminatory in relation to that person's protected characteristic.[19] A PCP is discriminatory in relation to a relevant protected characteristic of B if—

(a) A applies, or would apply, the PCP to persons with whom B does not share the characteristic,
(b) it puts, or would put, persons with whom B shares the characteristic at a particular disadvantage when compared with persons with whom B does not share it,
(c) it puts, or would put, B at that disadvantage, and
(d) A cannot show it to be a proportionate means of achieving a legitimate aim.[20]

Direct discrimination is simply illegal, except possibly in some very limited circumstances on grounds of age, but *indirect* discrimination can be permissible, *always provided that the employer can demonstrate that there was an objective justification for the PCP that it applied to its employees*. But to prove justification, the employer must show that there was no reasonable, less discriminatory alternative to the course of action pursued.

So, for example, it would be *indirectly* discriminatory for an employer to enforce a dress-code that excluded people who wore particular items of clothing for reasons of religion unless that employer could demonstrate that the dress-code was necessary for the proper performance of the job at hand—for example, on grounds of health and safety—and that there was no less-intrusive means of achieving the desired outcome. Religious sensibilities surrounding dress-codes caused considerable controversy when the National Health Service introduced the 'bare below the elbows' rule from January 2008 as part of more rigorous infection control. Muslim women objected on the grounds that they regarded bared arms as immodest—and the rule was subsequently amended to accommodate their concerns (Gainsbury, 2010).

18 (Advisory Conciliation and Arbitration Service, 2014: 3).
19 S.19(1).
20 S.19(2).

Furthermore, for behaviour to be indirectly discriminatory on grounds of religion, it must put employees in a particular religious group at disadvantage compared with their non-religious colleagues.

But those bald statements raise several complex issues in relation to religion and employment. First, to what extent may a worker in a secular organisation manifest his or her religious beliefs in the workplace? Secondly, to what extent may an overtly-religious organisation impose its own practices and ethos on its employees—and, indeed, to what extent is it allowed to make that a condition of employment in the first place? Thirdly, what happens when the protected characteristic of religion comes into conflict with another protected characteristic: sexual orientation, say, or marriage and civil partnership? (Vickers: 2015, 271–274).

Naeem was one of two conjoined cases—reported as *Essop*[21]—on the interpretation of indirect discrimination as defined in s.19 of the Equality Act 2010. Mr Naeem, a Muslim prison chaplain, relied on both race and religion—'but primarily religion' [3]. His claim was about the effect of the Prison Service pay scheme, which relates pay to length of service [12]. He became a salaried employee in 2004 and when he began proceedings, in April 2011, Muslim chaplains were paid, on average, £2,000 less than Christians because Muslims had only been salaried employees since 2002; however, a Christian chaplain with the same appraisal record who had started on the same day as Mr Naeem would be paid the same [14]. The Employment Tribunal ['ET'] had held that the pay scheme was indirectly discriminatory but objectively justified, while the Employment Appeal Tribunal ['EAT'] had held that the pay scheme was *not* indirectly discriminatory because chaplains employed before 2002 should be excluded from the comparison.

There were three issues: whether Mr Naeem had been disadvantaged because of his religion or race, whether the comparison should be with *all* prison chaplains or only those employed from 2002, and whether the EAT was entitled to interfere with the decision of the ET at all [16]. The Supreme Court dismissed the appeal, largely on the grounds that the findings of an ET on a matter of fact could not be questioned: in doing to, however, Lady Hale DPSC helpfully set out the 'salient features' of indirect discrimination:

- There is no express requirement for an explanation of the reasons *why* a particular PCP puts one group at a disadvantage when compared with others: 'It is enough that it does' [24].
- 'Direct discrimination expressly requires a causal link between the less favourable treatment and the protected characteristic. Indirect discrimination

21 *Essop & Ors v Home Office (UK Border Agency)* [2017] UKSC 27.

does not. Instead, it requires a causal link between the PCP and the particular disadvantage suffered by the group and the individual' [25].
- one group may find it harder than another to comply with the PCP for many reasons and 'the reason for the disadvantage need not be unlawful in itself or be under the control of the employer or provider (although sometimes it will be)' [26].
- 'there is no requirement that the PCP in question put *every* member of the group sharing the particular protected characteristic at a disadvantage' [27].
- statistical evidence shows correlations between particular variables and particular outcomes, 'But a correlation is not the same as a causal link' [28].
- 'it is always open to the respondent to show that his PCP is justified' [29].

In short, the judgment reaffirmed that indirect discrimination is about 'equality of *results*', not 'equality of *treatment*'.[22]

Harassment and Victimisation

Finally, there are the issues of harassment and victimisation. Under the terms of s.26(1) of the Equality Act 2010, harassment occurs in relation to a protected characteristic—in this case, religion or belief—when a person (A) harasses another (B) by engaging in unwanted conduct related to that characteristic and the conduct has the purpose or effect of violating B's dignity or creating an intimidating, hostile, degrading, humiliating or offensive environment for B.

Victimisation under s.27 of the 2010 Act occurs when a person (A) subjects another person (B) to a detriment because B does a protected act, or A believes that B has done, or may do, a protected act. Protected acts include: bringing proceedings under the Act, giving evidence or information in connection with proceedings under the Act, doing any other thing for the purposes of or in connection with the Act, and making an allegation (whether or not express) that A or another person has contravened the Act. Giving false evidence or information or making a false allegation are *not* protected if the evidence or information is given or the allegation made in bad faith.

Harassment and victimisation under the Equality Act are civil matters. In addition, however, the Protection from Harassment Act 1997, primarily intended to tackle so-called 'stalking', created the *criminal* offence of harassment.

---

22 In *Miss M Keens-Betts v The Anthony Gregg Partnership Ltd* [2017] UKET 2208102/2016, the Employment Tribunal held that there was no evidence that the claimant would have been treated any differently if she had not been a Christian because the generalised bullying culture of which she complained did not put Christian employees at a particular disadvantage compared with non-Christians: it affected them all equally [15 & 16].

Under that Act, harassment occurs where a person, A, engages in unwanted conduct related to the protected characteristic of religion or belief that has the purpose or effect of alarming a person, B, or causing that person distress.[23] An employer may be vicariously liable for a course of conduct by one of its employees that amounts to the offence of harassment under the 1997 Act;[24] the general issue of vicarious liability is discussed further below.

Employment Status: Employees, Workers and Office Holders

S.230(1) of the Employment Rights Act 1996 defines an 'employee' as 'an individual who has entered into or works under (or, where the employment has ceased, worked under) a contract of employment' and s.230(2) further defines 'contract of employment' as 'a contract of service or apprenticeship, whether express or implied, and (if it is express) whether oral or in writing'.

S.230(3) defines a 'worker' as 'an individual who has entered into or works under (or, where the employment has ceased, worked under) a contract of employment, or any other contract, whether express or implied and (if it is express) whether oral or in writing, whereby the individual undertakes to do or perform personally any work or services for another party to the contract whose status is not, by virtue of the contract, that of a client or customer of any profession or business undertaking carried on by the individual'. Therefore, a person is generally classed as a 'worker' if:

- he or she has a contract or other arrangement, whether written or verbal, to do work or services personally for reward;
- the reward is for money or a benefit in kind: for example, the promise of a contract or future work;
- he or she has only a limited right to send someone else to do the work;
- he or she has fixed hours of work;
- the employer has work for that person to do for as long as the contract or arrangement lasts; and
- the work is not being performed by the person's own limited company in an arrangement under which the 'employer' is actually a customer or client. (HM Government. nd, s.2: worker).

---

23 S.7(2) Protection from Harassment Act 1997. S.32 of the Crime and Disorder Act 1998 further provides that a person who commits an offence under s.2 or s.4 of the Protection from Harassment Act which is 'racially or religiously aggravated' within the meaning of s.28 of the Crime and Disorder Act 1998, as amended, is guilty of an offence triable either way.

24 *Majrowski v Guy's and St Thomas' NHS Trust* [2006] UKHL 34.

The distinction between the two is important because 'workers' have more limited employment rights than do 'employees'. Unlike 'employees', 'workers' do not normally have a right to a minimum notice period if their employment will be ending (for example, if the employer is dismissing them), protection against unfair dismissal, the right to request flexible working, time off for emergencies or Statutory Redundancy Pay (HM Government. nd, s.2 'worker').

'Office holders' are different again: as we shall see, they are not regarded as being employed in the sense of having employment rights. As to the distinction between 'employees', 'workers' and 'office holders', an 'office' has been defined as:

> a position of a public nature, filled by successive incumbents, whose duties were defined not by agreement but by law or by the rules of the institution.[25]

The Employment Status of Ministers of Religion

The courts have tended to regard clergy (and certainly beneficed clergy of the Church of England and inducted parish ministers of the Church of Scotland) as 'office holders' rather than as 'employees' or 'workers'. Furthermore, the status of ministers of religion has traditionally been regulated primarily, though not exclusively, by the internal canonical regulations of the denomination concerned. Historically, therefore, the courts have tended to proceed from three principles:

- that clergy are normally to be regarded as ecclesiastical office holders whose rights and duties are defined not by an employment contract but by the law relating to the office held, which exists independently of the person occupying that office;
- that the functions of clergy are vocational and spiritual in nature and therefore incompatible with the existence of a contract: on that view, they arise by way of a religious act such as ordination, not as the result of a contractual agreement between parties; and
- that even if there is evidence of some kind of contract, that evidence has to point to it being a contract *of employment*.

---

25 *President of the Methodist Conference v Preston* [2013] UKSC 29 at [4] *per* Lord Sumption JSC. His next sentence was 'A beneficed clergyman of the Church of England is, or was until recent measures modified the position, the paradigm case of a religious office holder'—a matter to which we shall return.

That said, however, the recent cases suggest that the position is not as clear-cut as the foregoing might suggest and that the precise employment situation of any individual minister is highly sensitive to the facts of the individual case.

The Employment Status of Ministers of Religion: The Case-Law

Churches and Faith-Communities Other Than the Church of England

As we shall see, in terms of employment law, the Church of England is something of a special case and it is therefore treated separately below. Whether clergy of other denominations in pastoral charges are 'employees', however, appears to depend at least to some extent on the ecclesiology and self-understanding of the particular Church in question. Fundamental to that are two fairly recent cases—*Percy*[26] and *Preston*[27]—but in order to put them in context, it is necessary to look at the earlier case-law which, in relation to status of clergy of denominations other than the Church of England, was somewhat equivocal.

The Earlier Cases

In *Parfitt*,[28] the respondent, a Methodist minister, failed in a claim for unfair dismissal before both an Employment Appeal Tribunal and the Court of Appeal, which held that the doctrinal standards of the Methodist Church did not provide for a contractual relationship between the Church and the individual minister. May LJ adopted the *dicta* of Waterhouse J in the EAT, as follows:

> The concept of a minister as a person called by God, a servant of God and the pastor of His [ie, presumably, God's] local church members seems to me to be central to the relationship. [186G]

In *Brentnall*,[29] however, the pursuer, a minister of the Free Presbyterian Church of Scotland, had been suspended *sine die*—in effect, dismissed—after proceedings in the Church's Synod which, he averred, had been *ultra vires* and contrary to the rules of natural justice. The Inner House of the Court of Session

26 *Percy v Church of Scotland Board of National Mission (Scotland)* [2005] UKHL 73; and see note 4 above.

27 *President of the Methodist Conference v Preston* [2013] UKSC 29.

28 *President of the Methodist Conference v Parfitt* [1984] ICR 176.

29 *Brentnall v Free Presbyterian Church of Scotland* 1986 SLT 471.

found for Mr Brentnall. It did not even begin to consider whether or not he was 'employed' by the Church: following the much earlier case of *Forbes*,[30] it was simply regarded as a matter of principle that if a wrongful act by the Church had caused him financial loss he must be entitled to reparation.

In *Davies*,[31] Lord Templeman reiterated the 'servant of God' approach and concluded:

> The duties owed by the pastor to the church are not contractual or enforceable. A pastor is called and accepts the call. He does not devote his working life but his whole life to the church and his religion. His duties are defined and his activities are dictated not by contract but by conscience. *He is the servant of God.* If his manner of serving God is not acceptable to the church, then his pastorate can be brought to an end by the church in accordance with the rules. The law will ensure that a pastor is not deprived of his salaried pastorate save in accordance with the provisions of the book of rules but an industrial tribunal cannot determine whether a reasonable church would sever the link between minister and congregation. [289C-E: emphasis added]

In *Buckley*,[32] a Roman Catholic priest in Northern Ireland sought a declaration that he had been removed unlawfully from his position. Campbell J held that because the Roman Catholic Church was a voluntary association, its clergy were bound in contract to the provisions of its canon law relating to their status. Given the terms of Canons 265 to 275 (on incardination) of the *Codex Iuris Canonici 1983*, he concluded that Lord Cranworth's *dictum* in the House of Lords in *Forbes* applied to the present case:

> There is no direct power in the courts to decide whether A or B holds a particular station according to the rules of a voluntary association.[33]

30 *Forbes v Eden* (1865) 4 M 143, an action against the Primus and General Synod of the Scottish Episcopal Church in which Lord Cowan declared that the courts would not review the actings of ecclesiastical judicatories unless 'Some civil wrong justifying a demand for redress, or some patrimonial injury entitling the party to claim damages ... be alleged and instructed' [163]—the 'patrimonial interest' being loss of stipend.

31 *Davies v Presbyterian Church of Wales* [1986] ICR 280.

32 *Buckley v Cahal Daly* [1990] NIJB 8.

33 *Forbes v Eden* [1867] 1HL Sc and Div 568 at 588.

Percy

I have already referred to Lord President Rodger's *dicta* in *Percy* on the relationship between the law of the Church of Scotland and Scots law generally, but the importance of the case for the present discussion is primarily in relation to clergy employment.

The Revd Helen Percy, an associate minister, was accused of adultery.[34] Rather than face trial by libel before her presbytery,[35] she was persuaded to demit status as a minister;[36] however, she later regretted that decision and initiated proceedings in an Employment Tribunal (then known as an Industrial Tribunal) in 1998, alleging unfair dismissal and unlawful sex discrimination.

The traditional view of the Church has been that an inducted parish minister is an office holder rather than an employee or a worker[37]—though that does not necessarily apply to Church of Scotland clergy in other positions. Ms Percy, however, was *not* an inducted parish minister but an associate: she was also a part-time chaplain at HM Prison Noranside. So there were three main issues before the Court:

- whether she was employed under a contract of employment;
- if she was *not* so employed, whether her relationship with the Church was still 'employment' as defined in s.82(1) of the Sex Discrimination Act 1975[38] and whether s.6 of that Act protected her from unlawful discrimination in the form of a more severe discipline than the Church was accustomed to impose on male ministers in similar circumstances; and
- whether, even if she *had* been discriminated against, her claim related to a 'matter spiritual' and therefore within the exclusive cognisance of the courts of the Church under s.3 of the Church of Scotland Act 1921.

---

34 She subsequently claimed that she had in fact been raped (Percy, 2011: 69–71, 76).

35 Under trial by libel, charges of misconduct by ministers were heard and determined by the members of the presbytery of the bounds rather than by a separate disciplinary tribunal. The Church of Scotland abolished it by Act III 2001 (Discipline of Ministry); however, the Free Church of Scotland still retains it (Free Church of Scotland, 2014: ch V). Whether or not trial by libel is compliant with Article 6 ECHR (right to a fair trial) is a very moot point indeed.

36 Which meant that she could not be reinstated and undertake duties as a minister except with the express agreement of the General Assembly.

37 HMRC's guidance says that 'Ministers of the Church of Scotland hold offices. However, they are not in employment'.

38 'In this Act, unless the context otherwise requires ... "employment" means employment under a contract of service or of apprenticeship or a contract personally to execute any work or labour, and related expressions shall be construed accordingly ...'.

The s.3 claim need not concern us here; but on the employment point, a majority of the House of Lords concluded that whether or not she was 'employed'—and therefore within the scope of the Sex Discrimination Act 1975—rested on a false dichotomy between 'office' and 'employment'. In the Inner House, Lord President Rodger had stated that he would

> start from the presumption—rebuttable, of course—that, where the appointment was being made to a recognised form of ministry within the Church and where the duties of that ministry would be essentially spiritual, there would be no intention that the arrangements made with the minister would give rise to obligations enforceable in the civil law.[39]

The majority rejected Lord Rodger's rebuttable presumption. Said Lord Nicholls of Birkenhead:

> If 'office' is given a broad meaning, holding an office and being an employee are not inconsistent. A person may hold an 'office' on the terms of, and pursuant to, a contract of employment ... Whether there is a contract in a particular case, and if so what is its nature and what are its terms, depends upon an application of familiar general principles. That the appointment in question is or may be described as an 'office' is a matter to be taken into account. The weight of this feature will depend upon all the circumstances. *But this feature does not of itself pre-empt the answer to the question whether the holder of the 'office' is an employee.* This feature does not necessarily preclude the existence of a parallel contract for carrying out the duties of the office even where they are statutory [20: emphasis added].

It was therefore possible in certain circumstances for a minister of religion to be in a contractual relationship with the Church as an employee. Moreover, absent any express intention to do so—and there had been no such express intention on the Church's part in relation to Ms Percy—the provisions of the Sex Discrimination Act 1975 could not be set aside. By entering into a contract for services, the parties had brought the relationship within the civil law and had taken it outside the exclusive jurisdiction of the church courts, so the provisions of the Church of Scotland Act 1921 no longer applied. The case was remitted to an Employment Tribunal but was ultimately settled.[40]

---

39 *Percy v Board of National Mission of the Church* [2001] ScotCS 65 at [13].

40 For a full discussion see Cranmer and Peterson (2006) and Lyall (2016: 80–82).

Stewart and *Macdonald*

In *Stewart*,[41] the claimant had been removed from his pastorate after accusations of financial irregularity and the Court of Appeal held that the original Employment Tribunal had been entitled to conclude on the facts that he had a contract of employment with the Church. However, Pill LJ was careful to add that his conclusion did not

> involve a general finding that ministers of religion are employees. Employment tribunals should carefully analyse the particular facts, which will vary from church to church, and probably from religion to religion, before reaching a conclusion [55].

The approach suggested by Pill LJ in *Stewart* was followed by the EAT in *Macdonald*.[42] The Revd Allan Macdonald had been suspended *sine die* by the Synod of the Free Presbyterian Church for breach of discipline and claimed unfair dismissal. Lady Smith, sitting alone, considered the possibility that a worker who was an office holder might also be an employee and concluded that the duality of holding an office while at the same time being in an employment relationship depended on whether or not the parties had had the intention to create legal relations [55]. She agreed with the ET that ministers, elders and deacons of the Church were ordained on an understanding that did not include any intention to create an employer-employee relationship; to conclude otherwise would be inconsistent with the Church's declared belief as set out in the *Manual and Practice of the Free Presbyterian Church* that it was inappropriate that officers such as ministers should be in a legal relationship that was subject to control by the Civil Magistrate [68].

Lady Smith held that there was no general rule either that all ministers of religion *were* employees or that they *were not* employees. She noted that, in *Stewart*, Pill LJ had been careful to state that whether or not there was an employer-employee relationship in a particular case depended on the facts. There were no hard-and-fast rules about what features a relationship had to have before it amounted to a contract of employment; but it would normally include, as a minimum, a mutual intention to create a legally-enforceable relationship and sufficient control over the worker's activities as to categorise him

41 *New Testament Church of God v Stewart* [2007] EWCA Civ 1004.

42 *Macdonald v Free Presbyterian Church of Scotland* [2010] UKEAT 0034/09/1002.

as a 'servant'—and the worker would be working in return for a salary rather than on his own account [63].[43] She dismissed the appeal.

Two problems should be noted in relation to the EAT judgment in *Macdonald*. First, the dispute was the subject of parallel judicial review proceedings in the Court of Session,[44] in which Mr Macdonald averred that he had been subjected over a period of two years or more to proceedings that had been conducted irregularly and unfairly and had ultimately led to his deposition from the ministry and the loss of his income, pension rights and accommodation [20]. In a preliminary judgment, the Lord Ordinary [Glennie] put the case out By Order to consider further procedure[45] [30]; but in September 2010 the case was settled out of court. Secondly, the pursuer's averments, both before Lady Smith in the EAT and before Lord Glennie in the Outer House, show a striking similarity to those in *Brentnall*—but neither judgment made any reference to the earlier case. Either *Brentnall* was never brought to their attention or they decided that it was irrelevant and not worth a mention.[46]

Preston

The Revd Haley Preston (*née* Moore) was removed from her post as Superintendent Minister of Redruth Circuit and sued the Methodist Conference. The ET had regarded itself as bound by *Parfitt* and dismissed her claim. In *Moore*,[47] however, the EAT reversed the lower tribunal's decision, concluding that it had been wrong in law. The EAT did not believe that the reasoning in *Parfitt* could be sustained in the light of *Percy*, even on the same facts [54]. Given that the EAT did not regard itself as bound by *Parfitt*, it chose to follow *Percy* and held that, on the facts, her contract was one of service. It noted that she received a regular stipend including an entitlement to sick pay, she was given accommodation, she was required to engage in an appraisal process, she was subject

43 *Ready Mixed Concrete (South East) Limited v Minister of Pensions & National Insurance* [1968] 1 AER 433 and *Lee v Chung and Shun Shing Construction & Engineering Co Ltd* [1990] IRLR 236 followed.

44 *Macdonald, Re Application for Judicial Review* [2010] ScotCS CSOH 55.

45 In essence, sent the case back to the parties for further explanation and submissions.

46 It should also be noted that Lady Smith reported without further comment (and, by implication, appeared to accept) the statement by Employment Judge Mackenzie about 'it being accepted that the Church of England recognises its clergy as being employees' [41], seemingly in contrast to the position adopted by the Free Presbyterian Church. Judge Mackenzie was wrong: as we shall see, the Church of England does *not* recognise clergy as employees, whether they have freehold or are on common tenure (which accounts for the vast majority of them).

47 *Moore v President of the Methodist Conference* [2010] UKEAT 0219/10/1503.

to at least a degree of supervision from the Church and she was liable to a disciplinary procedure [63]. The EAT also noted that, though she did not have set hours of work, there was a clear concept of working time and holidays, and though she had a great deal of discretion as to how she did her work, that was not inconsistent with a contract of service [63].

That decision was appealed; and in *Preston*[48] (Ms Moore having married in the meantime) the Court of Appeal unanimously upheld the EAT's finding. It concluded that it was 'abundantly clear' [21] that part of the conclusion in *Percy* had been to abandon the rebuttable presumption that there was no intention to create an employer/employee relationship between a Church and its clergy. The effect of *Percy* was that the spiritual role of a minister could not *of itself* justify denying recognition of an arrangement that otherwise had the marks of a contract: moreover, *Percy* had undermined the reasoning in the earlier case of *Parfitt*. Said Maurice Kay LJ:

> although most of the speeches in *Percy* are characterised by a linguistic gentleness in their approach to *Parfitt*, that does not disguise the fact that they caused the tectonic plates to move [25].

On appeal to the Supreme Court, however, the decision of the Court of Appeal was reversed and the original order of the Employment Tribunal dismissing Mrs Preston's claim restored. The Court held by four to one—Lady Hale JSC dissenting—that a Methodist minister was *not*, in fact, an employee. Under the Constitution and Standing Orders of the Methodist Church:

- a minister's engagement was incapable of being analysed in terms of contractual formation and neither admission to full connexion nor ordination was itself contractual;
- a minister's duties were not consensual but depended on the unilateral decisions of the Conference;
- stipend was paid and a manse provided by virtue only of admission into full connexion or ordination;
- stipend and manse were not remuneration for employment but 'a method of providing the material support to the minister without which he or she could not serve God';
- disciplinary rights under the Church's Deed of Union were the same for ordinary members of the Church as for ministers; and

48 *President of the Methodist Conference v Preston* [2011] EWCA Civ 1581.

- the relationship between the Church and the minister was terminable only by Conference, its Stationing Committee or by a disciplinary committee and there was no unilateral right to resign, even on notice [20].

Therefore, unless there was some special arrangement, a minister's rights and duties arose from his or her status under the Church's Constitution rather than under contract [20]. As to the judgment in *Percy*, the statutory test of 'employment' for the purposes of sex discrimination claims was broader than the test for unfair dismissal claims [7].

The Effects of *Preston*

If, as suggested by Maurice Kay LJ in *Preston*, the decision in *Percy* had 'caused the tectonic plates to move', Lord Sumption's judgment in the Supreme Court gave them a fairly firm shove in the opposite direction; and the result has been somewhat to clarify the employment position of ministers of religion outside the Church of England.

Both *Preston* and the EAT judgment in *Macdonald* suggest that whether or not an employer/employee relationship exists will depend on the Court's reading of the specific facts in the individual case and, at least to some extent, on the ecclesiology and doctrine of ministry of the Church concerned—or as Lord Sumption put it:

> Part of the vice of the earlier authorities was that many of them proceeded by way of abstract categorisation of ministers of religion generally. *The correct approach is to examine the rules and practices of the particular church and any special arrangements made with the particular minister* [26: emphasis added].

Recently, in *Celestial Church of Christ*,[49] a dispute arose as to the status of the pastor of a Church founded in the Republic of Benin in 1947 and incorporated in Nigeria in 1958 [2]. After the deaths of the founder and his immediate successor, a dispute over the subsequent succession led to a schism; and when some parishioners became unhappy with the pastorate of the Revd Mr Lawson, the issue arose as to the true meaning and effect of the Parish's constitution—which HHJ Hodge QC, sitting as a judge of the High Court, described at [19] as 'an unsatisfactory document in many respects which ... could have been clearer'—and whether the provisions of the worldwide constitution

49 *Celestial Church of Christ, Edward Street Parish (A Charity) v Lawson* [2017] EWHC 97 (Ch).

of the Celestial Church could be allowed to affect the interpretation of the governing constitution of the Parish.

HHJ Hodge ruled that they could not, still less could they be treated as part of it, because many of its provisions were at odds with the terms of the Parish's constitution [29]. He concluded that the ultimate power of appointment and dismissal was vested in the Parochial Committee [29] and that—crucially for the present discussion—following *Preston*, Mr Lawson was an office holder rather than an employee and his remuneration was properly to be viewed as stipend rather than salary [34].[50]

Similarly in *Harii*,[51] Employment Judge Pearl held that there was no contract of employment between a Baptist minister and his congregation because congregations in association with the Baptist Union of Great Britain 'have not employed ministers, they treat them as office holders and the Recommended Terms, for both part-time and full-time ministers, make this clear' and 'the absence of any of the usual "control" rules out an employment relationship' [30]. He accepted that the parties had not intended that the 'benefits and burdens' of the ministry were to be the subject of a contractually binding agreement between them.

The European Court of Human Rights and *Károly Nagy*

The approach of the courts in *Macdonald* and *Preston* has also been given a degree of support by a recent judgment of the European Court of Human Rights ('ECtHR') in *Károly Nagy*.[52] Mr Nagy, a minister in the Hungarian Reformed Church, brought a compensation claim following his dismissal as minister of Gödöllő parish after disciplinary proceedings in the ecclesiastical courts. His attempt to bring proceedings failed before both the labour courts and the ordinary civil courts: both sets of proceedings were ultimately discontinued for lack of jurisdiction and in May 2009 the Supreme Court concluded that his claim had no basis in civil law because there was no contractual relationship between him and the Church.

---

50 On the subsidiary point of Mr Lawson's removal as a trustee of the parish *ex officio*, he held that he had ceased to be a trustee, member or officer of the parish—and even had that not been the case, he would have exercised the court's jurisdiction to remove Mr Lawson as a charity trustee because to do so was necessary for the furtherance of the parish's charitable objectives [39].

51 *Rev T Harii v Tasso Baptist Church and London Baptist Association* [2017] UKET 2206435/2016.

52 *Károly Nagy v Hungary* [2015] ECHR 1051.

The Second Section dismissed his claim by a majority of four to three, holding that the Supreme Court had been within its powers to conclude that, though Mr Nagy could make a claim under ecclesiastical law before the relevant bodies of the Reformed Church, such a claim would not come within the jurisdiction of the secular courts [73]. Moreover, it held that excluding claims based on ecclesiastical law from the jurisdiction of domestic courts did not violate Article 6 §1 ECHR (right to a fair trial) [73].[53]

On appeal, the Grand Chamber agreed, holding by ten votes to seven that the application was inadmissible.[54] The fact that, under s.15(2) of Hungary's Church Act 1990, claims involving the internal laws and regulations of a denomination could not be enforced by organs of the state was not disputed. Furthermore, the parties agreed that, should the domestic courts establish that a dispute was about an ecclesiastical claim unenforceable by the domestic courts, they were obliged by Article 130(1)(f) of the Code of Civil Procedure to terminate the proceedings: 'The main question that arose before the domestic courts therefore revolved around the exact nature of the applicant's relationship with the Reformed Church' [66].

Under Mr Nagy's Letter of Appointment, he was to perform 'tasks defined by ecclesiastical laws and legal provisions … and the [relevant] code of conduct'. The Church's statutes provided that its relationship with its pastors should be governed by ecclesiastical law and that legal disputes over matters such as appointment, remuneration and retirement came within the jurisdiction of the ecclesiastical courts [68]. However, instead of taking his claim to the ecclesiastical courts, Mr Nagy had gone to the labour court, claiming that his relationship with the Church was akin to employment. When the labour court discontinued the proceedings on the grounds that his claim was unenforceable before them, instead of applying to the Supreme Court for review he had

53 Previously, in *Dudová and Duda v Czech Republic* [2001] ECHR No. 40224/98, the Court had declared inadmissible an application lodged by two former clergy of the Hussite Church who had sought to challenge the decision of their diocesan council to dismiss them, concluding that their claim did not relate to an arguable 'right' recognised by domestic law and that the complaint was therefore incompatible *ratione materiae*. In *Ahtinen v Finland* [2008] ECHR No 48907/99, the Court had held that the decision by the Church authorities to transfer a parish priest against his wishes did not engage Article 6, because under Finnish law the Evangelical Lutheran Church had the right to administer its own affairs and was independent in matters such as the appointment and service of its clergy; moreover, by agreeing to serve as a parish priest within the Church, the applicant had undertaken to abide by the rules incorporated in the Church Act 1993 and the Church Rules of Procedure [41].

54 *Károly Nagy v Hungary* [2017] ECHR 782.

turned to the secular courts and claimed that his relationship with the Church was an agency contract within the meaning of the Civil Code [69]. The first-instance civil court had concluded that it was not, because it lacked some of the important characteristics of an agency contract: in particular, the fact that his ecclesiastical services had no market value. The Supreme Court had confirmed that conclusion and had noted that his claim was ecclesiastical rather than civil and, therefore, unenforceable in the secular courts [70].

As to his claim under Article 6, all the domestic courts had examined his case in detail and concluded that it was governed by ecclesiastical rather than the secular law; and those findings were in line with the principles previously set out by the Constitutional Court [72]. S.15(2) of the Church Act 1990 was limited to issues involving the internal laws and rules of the Church in question and did not give Churches unfettered immunity against all civil claims [74]. However, his claim was of the kind that was excluded by s.15(2); and the domestic courts' conclusion that his pastoral service had been governed by ecclesiastical law was therefore neither arbitrary nor manifestly unreasonable [76]. So he had no 'right' that was recognisable under domestic law and 'To conclude otherwise would result in the creation by the Court, by way of interpretation of Article 6 §1, of a substantive right which had no legal basis in the respondent State' [77]. Article 6 was therefore inapplicable [78].

It is the Factual Situation that Determines the Relationship

Percy laid to rest the rebuttable presumption that where a Church appoints a minister to a post involving duties that will be essentially spiritual there is no intention of entering into contractual obligations enforceable in the secular law while, as Russell Sandberg points out (2014: 113–114), *Preston* explained how *Percy* related to the existing case-law and made clear that the reasoning in *Parfitt* was no longer good law.

But perhaps the most important feature of *Preston* is to emphasise that whether or not a contractual relationship exists between a Church and a minister in any particular case will depend on the precise factual situation—and the decision of the ECtHR in *Károly Nagy* lends further support to that view.

The Church of England

A Special Case?

The internal law of the Church of England is part of the general law of England (Doe, 1998: 17: Hill, 2007: 1.25 *et seq*) and its overall pattern of ministerial tenure—whether ordained or lay—shows a considerable degree of variation. Certain non-parochial clergy fulfilling specific functions for specific periods

(such as clergy employed as chaplains by NHS Trusts) are undoubtedly employed under contract; but they represent a relatively small proportion of the total body of clergy and, as to parochial clergy, the situation is quite different.

The classic position seems to have been that ministers of the Church of England could not be regarded as employees. In *Re National Insurance Act 1911*,[55] for example, it was held [at 568–9] that 'the position of curate is the position of a person who holds an ecclesiastical office, and not the position of a person whose duties and rights are defined by contract at all'. In *Barthorpe*,[56] however, in an EAT decision in which a stipendiary (lay) reader with the Mission to Seamen sued for unfair dismissal, Slynn J rejected the argument that an office holder could not be employed under a contract of service and added [906]:

> It may be difficult to establish who is the other contracting party, but we are not satisfied that clergy when working within the framework of the Church cannot be engaged under a contract. It may well be that the contract, if it exists, is for services rather than of service.

In *Coker*,[57] the Court of Appeal had to decide whether or not an assistant curate in the Church of England was an employee for the purposes of the unfair dismissal legislation. *Coker* has been largely superseded in relation to the Church of England itself; but Mummery LJ referred in his judgment to the case-law, including in particular *Parfitt* and *Davies*—to which reference was made earlier. His view was, in essence, that the earlier authorities had concluded that no contract of employment would normally arise between a minister of religion and his or her Church because, typically, *there was no intention to create contractual relations* [147B]. Staughton LJ concurred:

> in general, the duties of a minister of religion are inconsistent with an intention to create contractual relations. There may be some subsidiary contract as to a pension or to the occupation of a house; but there is not a contract that he will serve a terrestrial employer in the performance of his duties [150F-G].

55 *In re National Insurance Act 1911, On Employment of Church of England Curates* [1912] 2 Ch 563.

56 *Barthorpe v Exeter Diocesan Board of Finance* [1979] ICR 900.

57 *Diocese of Southwark v Coker* [1998] ICR 140.

Common Tenure

Since 2011, new appointments to incumbencies in the Church of England have tended to be made under the common tenure provisions of the Ecclesiastical Offices (Terms of Service) Measure 2009, rather than to freeholds.

Regulation 33 (right to apply to an employment tribunal) of the Ecclesiastical Offices (Terms of Service) Regulations 2009[58] has applied Part x of the Employment Rights Act 1996 to those who hold office under common tenure; however, the Regulations and the Measure confer rights under the 1996 Act *as if* such clergy were employed, not *because* they are employed. S.9(6) of the 2009 Measure makes that distinction explicit:

> Nothing in this Measure shall be taken as creating a relationship of employer and employee between an office holder and any other person or body.

Therefore, though clergy on common tenure have employment rights under the relevant legislation, *they are still not employees or workers but office holders.*[59] Furthermore, the position of parochial clergy with freehold (who, as we have already seen, have traditionally been regarded as office holders rather than as employees) remains unaffected by the Regulations and the Measure. The effect of the declaration in s.9(6) is to retain the historic distinction between the two categories and (presumably) to reduce what the Church might see as a risk that freehold incumbents could at some future date acquire employments rights by default.[60]

The *Sharpe* Litigation and the Employment Status of Incumbents

The Revd Mark Sharpe was Rector of Teme Valley South with freehold tenure. Relations with his parishioners deteriorated to such a degree that he retired on grounds of ill health, then sued the Diocesan Board of Finance (DBF) and the Bishop in his corporate capacity.[61] He presented two claims to an Employment

58 Which were made pursuant to s.2 of the Ecclesiastical Offices (Terms of Service) Measure 2009.

59 HMRC's current PAYE guidance (2016) declares that 'Ministers of the Church of England are office holders', while the Ecclesiastical Offices (Terms of Service) Directions 2010 (which confirm that clergy on common tenure are entitled to maternity, paternity and parental and adoption leave and have the right to request time off work or adjustments to their duties to care for a dependant) refer to 'the office holder'.

60 Non-parochial unbeneficed clergy in administrative or chaplaincy roles would normally have ordinary contracts of employment.

61 *Sharpe v Worcester Diocesan Board and the Bishop of Worcester* [2012] ET 1302291/2008.

Tribunal: that he had suffered detrimental treatment because he was a 'whistleblower' who had made protected disclosures and that he had been constructively and unfairly dismissed.

The ET pointed out that Mr Sharpe's position as a rector with freehold was defined by ecclesiastical law. Issues such as hours of work and holidays were left—non-contractually—to his discretion, subject only to guidelines as to how he exercised that discretion. Though the Diocese issued incumbents with something called the 'Bishop's Papers'—a kind of employees' handbook containing details of stipend and other financial matters—it could not be regarded as a contractual document.

There was no basis for finding that there had been a legal relationship between Mr Sharpe and the DBF: the DBF was not party to his appointment, it received no services from him, he carried out none on its behalf and it did not supervise him. Nor was there any contractual relationship between Mr Sharpe and the Bishop. It was the DBF that paid Mr Sharpe's stipend; the Bishop had no obligation to pay it, nor did he have control of the necessary funds to do so. The Bishop's powers of supervision were limited and were defined by law rather than by any consensual arrangement; moreover, they were mostly exercisable in the course of his statutory duties to ensure the proper running of his Diocese. The Bishop could not initiate disciplinary procedures of his own motion and, in any case, the statutory disciplinary procedures in the Clergy Discipline Measure 2003 were concerned primarily with the conduct of clergy *as clergy* rather than specific to their appointments.

In short, the Tribunal found that there was neither a contract of employment nor a contract of service: a general duty to obey the law of the Church was not the same as entering into a contract. The situation exhibited a lack of supervision and control and included no element of personal service: Mr Sharpe served the DBF and the Bishop only in the general sense of assisting the Church's mission. The claim was therefore dismissed.

In the EAT,[62] Cox J, sitting alone, overturned the Employment Tribunal:

> Following the decisions in both *Percy* and *Preston*[63] it is now abundantly clear that cases concerning the employment status of a minister of religion cannot be determined simply by asking whether the minister is an office holder or is in employment. As the Employment Judge recognised in this case, an individual appointed to work in a particular post may be

62 *Sharpe v Worcester Diocesan Board of Finance Ltd & Anor* [2013] UKEAT 0243/12/2811.

63 The Court of Appeal's ruling in favour of Mrs Preston that was subsequently reversed by the Supreme Court.

> both the holder of an office and an employee working under a contract of service. Whether there is payment of a salary, whether it is fixed, and whether the worker's duties are subject to the control of the employer are important matters to be considered in determining this issue [146].

Cox J concluded that the Tribunal's decision that Mr Sharpe was not a 'worker' within the meaning of s.230(3)(b) Employment Rights Act 1996 had been wrong. She allowed the appeal and remitted the case to the ET for a fresh hearing 'in accordance with the legal principles set out in this judgment' [244]. But before that could happen, in April 2015 the Court of Appeal unanimously reversed the EAT and restored the ruling of the Employment Judge.[64]

S.43K(1) of the Employment Rights Act 1996 extended the definition of 'worker' for the purpose of whistleblowing claims; and s.230 defines a 'worker' as someone with a contract of employment or who is to perform work or provide services for a third party. The primary focus of the appeal, therefore, was whether there was *in fact* a contract and, if so, whether it was a contract that fulfilled the requirements of ss.43(K)(1) and 230 in defining the relationship between Mr Sharpe and the Bishop.

The Court of Appeal concluded that the ET had found as a matter of fact that there was no contract, express or implied, between Mr Sharpe and the Bishop and held that there was no basis for setting aside that finding [80]; nor was Mr Sharpe an employee [81]. It held that the office of a freehold incumbent was 'governed by a regime which is a part of ecclesiastical law. *It is not the result of a contractual arrangement*' [108: emphasis added]. The element of control necessary for there to be an employer/employee relationship was not present: 'the opportunity for the hierarchy of the Church to intervene in the performance of duties [of a freehold incumbent] is reduced in practice to vanishing point or at least to the minimum' [109].

Licences to Minister

In the Church of England, any cleric 'wishing to exercise a public ministry other than in senior appointments or as incumbent must be granted either permission to officiate or a licence by the diocesan bishop' (Church of England, 2014). Therefore, associated with the issue of employment status are the rather more complex problems of licences to minister and permission to officiate ('PTO') and whether or not a diocesan bishop is a 'qualifications body' for the purposes of discrimination, harassment or victimisation.

---

64 *Sharpe v Bishop of Worcester* [2015] EWCA Civ 399.

S.53 Equality Act 2010 provides that a qualifications body (A) may not discriminate against, harass or victimise a person (B), while s.54(2) and (3) define a qualifications body as 'an authority or body which can confer a relevant qualification' and a 'relevant qualification' as 'an authorisation, qualification, recognition, registration, enrolment, approval or certification which is needed for, or facilitates engagement in, a particular trade or profession'.

In *Ganga*,[65] which concerned the revocation of the Revd Mr Ganga's licence on the grounds that he was so heavily in debt that he could no longer be regarded as 'fit and proper' to exercise ministry, an Employment Tribunal concluded that the Bishop of Chelmsford was indeed a qualifications body for the purposes of s.53—but dismissed the claim on other grounds.

The issue came up again in *Pemberton*.[66] Canon Jeremy Pemberton married Laurence Cunnington in April 2014 and in June 2014 the Acting Bishop of Southwell and Nottingham, Bishop Inwood, revoked his permission to officiate in his diocese. Sherwood Forest Hospitals NHS Trust had earlier offered Canon Pemberton the post of Chaplaincy and Bereavement Manager. The post had two elements: the NHS Trust would employ him but he would also need the necessary authorisation from the Church to function as a priest within the hospital context. In order to take up the position, therefore, he needed an Extra-Parochial Ministry Licence ('EPML') from the Bishop under the Extra-Parochial Ministry Measure 1967. However, the Bishop refused to grant him a licence because, in his view, his marriage was contrary to the teachings and law of the Church of England. In consequence, the NHS Trust withdrew its offer of employment—and Canon Pemberton sued under s.53 Equality Act 2010 for unlawful direct discrimination because of sexual orientation and/or marital status and unlawful harassment related to sexual orientation.

It was evidently common ground between the parties that the Church did not employ Canon Pemberton and that he could not, therefore, bring a claim under s.39 (Employees and applicants) of the 2010 Act. Moreover, the Bishop contended that he was not a qualifications body for the purposes of s.53 but that, if the Employment Tribunal should find to the contrary, because the qualification in question was 'for the purposes of employment for the purposes of organised religion' it would attract the saving under Schedule 9 para 2 (Religious requirements relating to sex, marriage etc., sexual orientation).

As in *Ganga*, the ET concluded that the Bishop was indeed a qualifications body for the purposes of s.53; however, the ET also found, on the facts, that a

---

65 *Ganga v Chelmsford Diocesan Board of Finance and the Bishop of Chelmsford in corporate capacity* [2015] ET 3200933/2013.

66 *Pemberton v Inwood, Acting Bishop of Southwell and Nottingham* [2015] ET 2600962/2014.

PTO was 'voluntary and not for remuneration' and that because it was not a *relevant* qualification it did not engage s.53.

The ET's reasons for dismissing the claim were that the present doctrine of the Church was that marriage was between one man and one woman and that, until there was a change in that doctrine, clergy had to conform to it in their ministry and individual behaviour. Given that Canon Pemberton's position was incompatible with that doctrine, it logically followed that the Bishop's action had been implicitly proportionate. It also dismissed the harassment claim. Canon Pemberton appealed and the Bishop cross-appealed.

In the EAT,[67] HHJ Eady dismissed both the appeal and the cross-appeal, which fell to be considered under three headings: qualifications bodies and the issue of 'relevant qualification'; the application of paragraph 2 schedule 9 Equality Act 2010; and the harassment claim [48].

The starting point for both the appeal and cross-appeal was whether the ET had been correct to hold that the Bishop *was not* a qualifications body in respect of the PTO (first ground of appeal) but *was* a qualifications body in respect of the EPML (first ground of cross-appeal). Both parties agreed that the Bishop would be a qualifications body for the purposes of s.53 *if he could properly be said to have conferred a 'relevant qualification' under s.54(3)* [49].

On the first issue, HHJ Eady upheld the ET's key finding that the Bishop had revoked Canon Pemberton's PTO because he regarded Canon Pemberton as no longer 'in good standing'. As to the cross-appeal, her view was that hospital chaplaincy was 'plainly a vocation or calling such as to meet the broad definition of "profession"': consequently, to grant a qualification for the purpose of a particular position that facilitated engagement in that profession met the requirements of s.54(3) [108]. Furthermore, the NHS Trust had been content to leave to the Bishop the decision as to whether or not approval would be given by way of an EPML; and the key point was that the body granting the qualification was not simply applying a standard for its own purposes but was signifying that the individual met a particular standard on which others would rely in granting access to a particular profession [108].

As to the application of paragraph 2 schedule 9 Equality Act 2010, Canon Pemberton had contended that the post in question was employment *within the NHS*, not within the Church, that the Trust's appointment of a chaplain was part of its overall health-care provision and that the Church of England played no part in setting the job description for the role nor in the selection of candidates [110]. HHJ Eady's answer was that the exception permitted by paragraph 2 of schedule 9 was not limited to employment within a religious

67 *Pemberton v Inwood* [2016] UKEAT 0072/16/0712.

organisation because it was not the nature of the organisation that was in issue *but the purpose of the employment.* Authorisation to minister as a Church of England priest was an essential requirement of the post and an integral part of what the Trust intended for the role [110]—and that was the purpose of the qualification that Canon Pemberton had sought. The licence was therefore 'for the purpose of employment for the purpose of an organised religion (here, the Church of England), albeit carried out whilst employed by a secular body' [111].

As to whether the ET had erred in concluding that the Bishop had applied a requirement that engaged the compliance principle for the purpose of paragraph 2(5) schedule 9, she held that the ET had been entitled to find that the doctrines of the Church of England were as stated by Canon B30[68] and, with specific regard to same-sex marriages as evidenced by the *Report of the House of Bishops' Working Group on human sexuality* and the Pastoral Guidance, that marriage for the purposes of the Church of England was *'between one man and one woman'* [112]. On that basis, the ET had been entitled to conclude that the Bishop had applied the requirement that Canon Pemberton should not be in a same-sex marriage so as to comply with that doctrine [113]. Furthermore:

> the fact that another Bishop might not have applied the same requirement does not take his decision outside sub-paragraphs 2(3) and (5). The exception allowed by paragraph 2 recognises that there may not be one consistent view within any religious community [114].

As to the harassment claim, she felt that though the ET could have chosen its words more carefully [123] there had been no error of law in its finding [124].

Having dismissed both the appeal and the cross-appeal, she concluded by stating that the matter was a suitable case for the Court of Appeal should an application for leave be made [126].[69]

Article 9 and the Rights of the Church

Coupled with the issue of clergy tenure is the right claimed by the Churches to order themselves in accordance with their own particular ecclesiology.

---

68 Canon B 30 (Of Holy Matrimony): '1. The Church of England affirms, according to our Lord's teaching, that marriage is in its nature a union permanent and lifelong, for better for worse, till death them do part, *of one man with one woman*, to the exclusion of all others on either side …' [emphasis added].

69 At the time of writing, it was not clear whether there would, in fact, be a further appeal: for the latest position, see Church of England (2017a).

In *Stewart*, Pill LJ addressed the relationship between Article 9 ECHR (freedom of thought, conscience and religion) and the self-understanding of particular denominations as follows:

> The religious beliefs of a community may be such that their manifestation does not involve the creation of a relationship enforceable at law between members of the religious community and one of their number appointed to minister to the others, whether the appointment is by the local congregation or under an episcopal form of government. *The law should not readily impose a legal relationship on members of a religious community which would be contrary to their religious beliefs.* These beliefs and practices may be such, in the context of a particular church, that no intention to create legal relations is present. To take them into account does not involve any departure from ordinary contractual principles, *especially in the light of Article 9* [47: emphasis added].

In the EAT hearing in *Macdonald*, Lady Smith noted that the ET had referred briefly to Article 9 and the fact that account had to be taken of the principles of an individual Church when determining whether or not there was an intention to create an employer/employee relationship:

> That is because the law should not readily impose on the members of a church a legal relationship that would be contrary to their religious beliefs, as discussed in *New Testament Church of God v Stewart* [42].

She concluded, however, that in the case before her the concern that the Church's Article 9 rights might have been breached was unnecessary.

The issue was raised in the Court of Appeal in *Preston* and was given very short shrift by Maurice Kay LJ:

> When asked to explain how the existence of a contract of employment might interfere with the right of Methodists to manifest their religious belief, [counsel] referred only to the implications of accountability in an ET and the financial cost involved. I am sorry to say that, to my mind, this only serves to emphasise the unattractiveness and moral poverty of the attempted invocation of Article 9 in this case. The EAT concluded ... that it is not a case where the evidence establishes that the existence of a contract of employment between the Church and a Minister is contrary to its tenets and it could not conceive that any claim within the jurisdiction

> of the ET would require it to determine disputed issues of doctrine. I entirely agree [34].

The point does not appear to have been argued subsequently before the Supreme Court.

So Where Next?

As noted above, *Percy* and *Preston* between them have clarified the law and re-emphasised the fact-specific nature of employment claims and the importance of courts and tribunals looking carefully at the intentions of the parties in determining whether or not an employment relationship exists.

As to the Church of England, the Ecclesiastical Offices (Terms of Service) Measure 2009 and the Ecclesiastical Offices (Terms of Service) Regulations 2009 are *de facto* recognition by the Church of the desirability of clergy holding office under common tenure having at least limited employment rights. But unless and until *Sharpe* is reversed, the dwindling number of clergy with the traditional freehold will continue to have no such rights at all—though, in fairness, it should be said that it is extremely difficult to remove a freehold incumbent from office.

Lay Employees, Interns, Volunteers and the Wider Picture

The Changing Patterns of Work and Employment

As noted in the Introduction, the basic model of an employment relationship is one of mutuality of obligations: a contract under which the employer provides work and controls how, when and where the work is done, in return for which the employee or worker performs the work in person and is paid for it. But changing patterns of work have led to a situation in which the old model of the 9-to-5, 48-week working year with a weekly pay packet or a monthly salary cheque is no longer necessarily the norm.

The growth in the numbers of interns, part-timers, work-experience students and volunteers has raised some difficult questions about their status. Twenty years ago, those distinctions were much more clear-cut; but changing patterns of work, the decisions of employment tribunals and the introduction of the National Minimum Wage and, subsequently, the National Living Wage (NMW/NLW) have all combined to blur the overall picture. Moreover, arbitrary labels are misleading: as we shall see, expressions such as 'internship' or 'work experience placement' have no status in law.

As noted earlier, the rights of people at work generally depend on their employment status: whether someone is an employee, a worker or an office holder. These categories are not necessarily mutually exclusive and every case falls to be determined on the facts. Furthermore, employment status may be classified differently according to whether the issue is one of tax or employment law: and with regard to the latter, establishing employment status is essential for accessing many employment rights such as protection from unfair dismissal.

Charities, in particular, make heavy use of part-time workers, interns and volunteers and their position in employment terms can be complex.

Is There a Contract of Employment or Service?

The Prison Act 1952 requires every prison in England and Wales to have a chaplain who must be a cleric of the Church of England or the Church in Wales;[70] in addition, however, the Home Office appoints assistant chaplains to minister to prisoners of their own faith. In *Miller*,[71] the claimant, a Quaker visiting minister at HM Prison Wymott, received hourly pay and expenses. She arranged services and ministered to inmates—and not just to Quakers—suffering emotional stress, attended meetings of the chaplaincy team, organised an Alternatives to Violence programme for inmates and sat on a number of prison committees. When a vacancy for a part-time chaplain arose, she covered some of those duties, including visiting prisoners in the segregation unit and on suicide watch and interviewing new arrivals: duties which fell to the statutory Church of England Chaplain under the terms of the Prison Act. However, the Home Office could not direct her as to how she carried out her work and, unlike the full-time Chaplain, she did not have targets set for her and was not subject to regular appraisals by the Governor or to the Home Office's disciplinary and grievance procedures.

In 2003, her appointment was summarily terminated and she claimed unfair dismissal. The question before the Employment Tribunal had been whether she was employed by the Home Office under a contract of service within the meaning of s.230 Employment Rights Act 1996. The EAT concluded that there was probably some kind of contract with Ms Miller but that she was not an employee because there were no enforceable obligations imposed on her and the necessary degree of control was absent. The EAT noted that the fact that she 'could simply withdraw from running the Alternative to Violence programme without demur by the Governor' [15] was inconsistent with a degree of control

70 S.7(1), s.7(4), s.53(3.

71 *Miller v Secretary of State for Home Affairs* [2004] UKEAT 00926 03 0405.

by the Home Office that was sufficient to imply a contractual employer/employee relationship.

Recently, there was a similar outcome in *Rahman*.[72] The claimant, a Muslim chaplain, began work in 2006 as a sessional chaplain at HM Prison Wormwood Scrubs, moving to HMP Brixton in 2010. He did not have a written contract, 'although the [Employment] Tribunal was shown an unsigned example of a contract for sessional chaplains, which emphasised the lack of mutual obligations' [13]. In 2010, he was promised that he would be made permanent; however, that did not happen, there was no change to his working pattern and he was not given a contract or any contractual benefits [15]. His claim was for discrimination on grounds of race and religion, unfair dismissal and a failure to make payments in respect of notice, sickness and holidays [1].

The Tribunal's conclusion was that sessional workers were not employees within the statutory definitions because there was no mutuality of obligation. A sessional chaplain did not work under a contract of employment but, rather, as an independent provider of particular services able to choose what he or she did or did not do, 'without sanction (apart from termination)'; nor was a sessional chaplain a worker [23]. Therefore, Mr Rahman was neither an employee as defined in the Employment Rights Act 1996 s.230(1) and (2) nor a worker as defined in s.230(3).

Rather more straightforward was *Piper*,[73] in which the EAT held that the lead chaplain of an NHS Trust could bring a claim for unfair dismissal. The EAT remitted the case to a different Tribunal for rehearing to determine that complaint on its merits—but it was not suggested that there was no employment relationship between the Revd Mr Piper and the Trust.

Likewise in *Singh*,[74] the issue was what constituted 'employment' in relation to church personnel—this time for the purposes of s.54(3)(b) National Minimum Wage Act 1998 (of which more below). *Singh* is a complex case, not least because any baptised Sikh in good standing can act as a *granthi*,[75] so it is not entirely clear that a *granthi* is on all fours with an ordained minister of religion. Moreover, the relationship between the parties was a voluntary one: Mr Singh did not have a formal written agreement with the Management Committee and he and his wife were supported by the voluntary contributions of the congregation and lived rent-free at the *gurdwara*. The original Employment Tribunal had therefore held that Mr Singh was not an employee.

---

72 *Rahman v Ministry of Justice* [2017] UKET 2300311/2016.

73 *Piper v Maidstone & Tunbridge Wells NHS Trust* [2012] UKEAT 0359 12 1812.

74 *Singh v Management Committee of the Bristol Sikh Temple & Ors* [2012] UKEAT 0429 11 1402.

75 A temple priest.

The EAT disagreed, concluding that the lower Tribunal had erred on the questions of mutuality and personal performance of services. Though the relationship was indeed based on 'voluntarism and a traditional interpretation and application of the Sikh scriptures' [39] there had been no finding that a contractual relationship would be inconsistent with the practice and beliefs of the Bristol Gurdwara. Crucially, the EAT took the view that the true effect of *Percy* had not been fully taken into account by the lower Tribunal—possibly, said Beatson J, 'because one result of what Maurice Kay LJ described [in *Preston*] as "a linguistic gentleness" in the approach of the judgments in *Percy* to the earlier decisions meant that the implications of that decision were not in fact fully appreciated' [40]. The appeal was allowed and the case remitted to the original Tribunal for reconsideration. It should be said that whether *Singh* would have been decided differently if it had been handed down after the Supreme Court judgment in *Preston* is a very moot point, given Lord Sumption's views on the scope of the decision in *Percy*—and the direction of travel in *Sharpe* was the same.

There was a somewhat similar outcome in *Chandra*.[76] In March 2011, Dr Chandra had been employed by the Executive Committee of Arya Samaj Vedic Mission to work at its temple on a twelve-month contract at £500 per month with a one-bedroom apartment and an arrangement that allowed him to receive commission based on those attending his courses. It turned out, however, that he was expected to spend a very large amount of his available time working and was provided only with a small single room. In March 2012, he was awarded a new three-year contract under the same terms and conditions; but in July 2012 the Executive Committee members stood down and were replaced by new members who, shortly afterwards, terminated Dr Chandra's new contract.

HHJ Purle QC concluded that since there was no clause in Dr Chandra's contract specifying the number of hours to be worked, his payment was therefore for 'unmeasured work' rather than a salary—and, in fact, he had ended up working a 65-hour week. The Executive Committee had therefore failed to pay him the NMW rate, even taking into account the statutory accommodation offset rate of £34.37 per week then prescribed by the National Minimum Wage Regulations. He was awarded just over £62,500 in damages.

Most recently, the Court of Appeal has underlined yet again the basic rule that *in order to have employment rights, the claimant must be in an employment relationship*. In a complex case of alleged religious discrimination in

76 *Chandra v Arya Samaj Vedic Mission (West Midlands)* [2014] Birmingham County Court (unreported).

employment, *Halawi*,[77] the claimant was a Christian who worked as a beauty consultant at Heathrow Terminal 3. She operated through her own limited company, Nohad Ltd; Nohad invoiced an intermediary agency for her time and services and the agency, in turn, invoiced World Duty Free. She alleged that she and other Christian staff had been systematically harassed by Muslim colleagues and that this had led to her losing her job when WDFG UK Ltd took away her airside pass—without which she could not function. She was unsuccessful both before the Employment Tribunal and the EAT, neither of which believed her claim.

The Court of Appeal agreed with the EAT, holding that because Mrs Halawi worked through Nohad Ltd and the intermediary agency she could not be a 'worker' or 'employee' for the purpose of discrimination in employment under s.83(2)(a) Equality Act 2010—which covers 'employment under a contract of employment, a contract of apprenticeship or a contract personally to do work'—so the issue of alleged religious discrimination fell away.

Can There be an Employment Relationship even if the Employer did not Intend to Create One?

In *Autoclenz*,[78] the Supreme Court confirmed the common law principle that the labels which parties attach to an arrangement are not determinative of employed status.

The claimants, who valeted cars on behalf of Autoclenz Ltd, had all signed statements declaring unequivocally that they were self-employed; and they were taxed on that basis rather than under PAYE. Nevertheless, they sought a declaration in an Employment Tribunal that they were, in reality, workers and were therefore entitled to holiday pay and the National Minimum Wage under the Working Time Regulations 1998 and the National Minimum Wage Regulations 1999. It was common ground between the parties that if the terms of the written declaration were valid then, as a matter of law, the claimants could not be 'workers' within the meaning of either set of Regulations.

The Supreme Court held unanimously that valeters *had*, in fact, been working under contracts of employment and that the ET had been entitled to hold that the documents did not reflect the true agreement between the parties and to disregard their terms insofar as they were inconsistent with the actual situation. Delivering the sole judgment, Lord Clarke agreed with the Court of Appeal's conclusions that the correct approach was to discover the parties' actual legal obligations:

---

77 *Halawi v WDFG UK Ltd (t/a World Duty Free)* [2014] EWCA Civ 1387.

78 *Autoclenz Ltd v Belcher & Ors* [2011] UKSC 41.

> The relative bargaining power of the parties must be taken into account in deciding whether the terms of any written agreement in truth represent what was agreed and the true agreement will often have to be gleaned from all the circumstances of the case, of which the written agreement is only a part. This may be described as a purposive approach to the problem. If so, I am content with that description [35].

In short, before *Autoclenz* the courts were bound by the terms of written contracts, always provided that those terms were not obviously designed to deceive; after *Autoclenz*, however, they can set aside express contractual terms that appear inconsistent with the reality of the parties' relationship without having to establish a common intention to mislead.[79]

The implications of all this for religious organisations are considerable. For example, there have been various recent cases on the employment status of church organists, of which perhaps the most important recent one is *Sholl*.[80]

Dr Sholl had been appointed Director of Music for a minimum of five years at an annual stipend of £14,000. The draft contract (which Dr Sholl did not sign) included the provisos in Clause 16 that 'There being no master and servant relationship [and] no part of this Agreement shall be deemed to constitute a contract of employment' and that 'The Director of Music shall be responsible for his own income tax and National Insurance arrangements' [28]. The unsigned draft contract also stated that 'subject to the general direction of the Vicar, the Director of Music shall be responsible for the care, control and general oversight of all the music in the Church' [45]. It also stated that the agreement was subject to the provisions of Canon B20 of the *Canons of the Church of England*[81] [46]. Though the contract was never signed, the Tribunal concluded

79 See, for example, Handley (2011). A recent case is *Aslam & Ors v Uber BV & Ors* [2016] UKET 2202500/2015, in which a group of drivers who carried passengers booking cars using the Uber smartphone app argued that, rather than being self-employed contractors, in reality they were working under Uber's control. The Employment Tribunal concluded that, whatever the ostensible terms under which Uber's drivers were engaged, they were workers for the purposes of the NMW/NLW, holiday pay and the like: 'The notion that Uber in London is a mosaic of 30,000 small businesses linked by a common "platform" is to our minds faintly ridiculous' [90].

80 *Sholl v PCC of St Michael & All Angels w St James, Croydon & Anor* [2011] ET 2330072/2010.

81 B 20 (Of the musicians and music of the Church) '1. In all churches and chapels, other than in cathedral or collegiate churches or chapels where the matter is governed by or dependent upon the statutes or customs of the same, the functions of appointing any organist, choirmaster (by whatever name called) or director of music, and of terminating the appointment of any organist, choirmaster or director of music, shall be exercisable by

that there was a verbal contract between the parties and that a sufficient element of control existed for it to be a contract to be one of service [53].

The Tribunal identified several factors consistent with a contract of employment: Dr Sholl was paid monthly in arrears; the payments 'clearly had the character of a contractual remuneration'; he had no financial risk; he was not required to provide equipment, materials or premises; he had a package of rights to holiday pay, sick pay and notice and grievance provisions; and the second respondent, the Vicar, had himself described Dr Sholl's status as 'employed' [61]. The principal factors against the presumption were that Dr Sholl had been informed that he was self-employed; he paid his own income tax and National Insurance; he delegated work to others outside the terms of the agreement; he did not obtain advance authorisation for annual leave; and he received separate fees for playing at weddings and funerals [62].

The Tribunal reminded itself of 'the well-established common law principle that the labels parties attach to the arrangement are not determinative of employed status' [65] and, on balance, it concluded that the factors in favour of employment status outweighed those against [67]. It agreed that the matter should proceed to a full merits hearing [74] but, in the end, the case was settled.

Interns and Volunteers

Religious organisations, like many others, have adopted the practice of offering internships, usually but not always to recent graduates. However, there is no legal definition of 'an intern'—and that can raise problems in relation to employment status in general and to entitlement to the NMW/NLW in particular. As Lord Wallace of Saltaire pointed out in answer to a Parliamentary Question from Lord Storey in January 2015:

> The term 'intern' is not defined in any legislation: entitlement to the minimum wage depends on whether or not an individual is a worker. If an internship meets the legal definition of a worker, then they must be paid at least the minimum wage from the start. Given the dependency on employment status, it is vital that employers and workers understand how this is determined.[82]

---

the minister with the agreement of the parochial church council ...' (Church of England, 2016). In February 2017, the Legal Advisory Commission of the General Synod published an opinion (Church of England, 2017b) on *The Parish Music: organists and choirmasters and church musicians* much of which, leaving aside the specific references to Canon B20, is equally applicable to other denominations.

82 HL Deb (2014–15) 6 Jan 2015 c WA221.

Doug Pyper (2015, 8) cites two employment cases in which an Employment Tribunal concluded that someone engaged as an intern *was* in fact a worker for the purposes of the NMW. In *Vetta*,[83] it was held that the claimant, who was engaged as an art department assistant for expenses only, was entitled to the NMW because mutual obligations existed between her and the defendant. Similarly, in *Hudson*,[84] an intern found herself working from 10 am to 6 pm and supervising a team; and the defendant had at one point considered paying her but had then decided against doing so. The ET concluded that a contract existed between Ms Hudson and TPG and that she was therefore entitled to be paid at least the NMW.

So, once more, the cases are highly fact-sensitive; however, the issue of the employment status of volunteers has been finally laid to rest by the Supreme Court judgment in *Mid Sussex CAB*.[85]

Ms X was a volunteer adviser with the Mid Sussex Citizens Advice Bureau. At her interview, it was explained that there would be no binding legal contract between her and the Bureau and she signed a volunteer agreement to that effect, headed 'This agreement is binding in honour only and is not a contract of employment or legally binding'. When she was told that her services were no longer required she sued, claiming that the actions of the CAB had amounted to discrimination against her on the grounds of disability, contrary to the Disability Discrimination Act 1995 and the Framework Directive. At an earlier stage in the proceedings, it became common ground between the parties that if Ms X was indeed protected by the disability discrimination legislation, then volunteers generally could be regarded as having employment rights.

The Court, however, would have none of it. Lord Mance, delivering the sole judgment, held that—in a nutshell—'the Framework Directive does not cover voluntary activity' [45] and dismissed the appeal. Moreover, he did not regard it as a case in which a reference to the Court of Justice of the EU was 'either required or appropriate' [57]. And there, for the moment, the matter rests.

The key point in relation to volunteers is that *they must be genuine volunteers*, paid no more than their legitimate expenses incurred as a result of volunteering. Once payment goes beyond reimbursing expenses, there is a serious danger than the courts might interpret the resulting relationship as one of employment, *even though there was no intention on the part of the organisation to create such a relationship*. Moreover, as Lucy McLynn and Victoria Cook point out (2016: 15), where an organisation sets up the same kind of structured

---

83 *Vetta v London Dreams Motion Pictures Ltd* [2010] ET 2703377/08.

84 *Hudson v TPG Web Publishing Ltd & Ors* [2011] ET 2200565/11.

85 *X v Mid Sussex Citizens Advice Bureau & Anor* [2012] UKSC 59.

relationship between itself and the volunteer that it would have had with a paid trainee or apprentice—such as a requirement about attendance—or where a volunteer is, in reality, *required* to carry out certain duties, volunteering starts to shade into employment—and it might then be very unwise to rely on *Mid Sussex* CAB.

Right to the National Minimum Wage/National Living Wage

The National Minimum Wage Act 1998, which came into effect on 1 April 1999, established a minimum wage for workers aged 18 and over. From 1 April 2016, the National Minimum Wage Regulations 2015 created an obligatory National Living Wage for workers aged 26 and over. In relation to eligibility of interns and those on work experience placements there are various considerations to be borne in mind:

- An intern with the status of a *worker* is entitled to the NMW/NLW; and an employer cannot avoid the duty to pay the NMW/NLW merely by stating that it does not apply or by concluding a written agreement stating that the person in question is not a worker or that that person is a volunteer.
- An intern is classed as a worker and is entitled to the NMW/NLW if he or she is promised a contract of future work.

Interns are *not* entitled to the NMW/NLW in the following circumstances:

- *Student internships:* a student required to undertake an internship for less than one year *as part of a UK-based further or higher education course* is not entitled to the NMW/NLW.
- *School work experience placements:* work experience students *of compulsory school age* (ie under 16) are not entitled to the NMW/NLW.
- *Work-shadowing*: the employer does not have to pay an intern the NMW/NLW if the internship *only* involves shadowing an employee, the intern is not carrying out any work and he or she is only observing the person being shadowed.

In addition, *volunteers* are not entitled to the NMW/NLW if they are *both* volunteering for a charity, a voluntary organisation, an associated fundraising body or a statutory body *and* are only paid limited benefits such as reasonable travel or lunch expenses.

But what would happen if, for example, a church appointed a part-time youth-worker and said to its new employee, 'Sorry: we can only afford to pay you the National Living Wage for twenty hours a week but you could work the rest of the week as a volunteer'? How might that play before an Employment Tribunal?

As implied above, the probability is that on the principle enunciated in *Autoclenz* of looking at the actual situation rather than the written or verbal agreement, an Employment Tribunal would need to be satisfied that any work over and above the contracted twenty hours *was in fact* genuinely voluntary and not merely a device to circumvent the NMW Regulations. That, in turn, would depend at least in part on the nature of the work. If, for example, a church youth-worker took occasional church services as a lay volunteer or ran part of the church's Sunday-school, a tribunal might take the view that that was the kind of activity that any committed member of a congregation might reasonably undertake without reward. If, on the other hand, a claimant did twenty hours of paid work a week followed by fifteen hours of 'more of the same', a tribunal might take the view that *the reality* was that the claimant was in fact working a 35-hour week for less than the NMW/NLW hourly rate—and that suggestion would appear to be supported by *Singh*, as noted above.

In short, the employment status of lay church-workers is by no means cut-and-dried; and just because a group of trustees says that it does not intend to 'employ' an organist, a choirmaster, a cleaner or a caretaker does not mean that no employment relationship exists. Furthermore, once one strays outside the traditional pattern of a contract of employment with tax paid through PAYE and the normal entitlements to such things as holiday pay and moves into the shadowy world of internships, voluntary work and expenses, employment law becomes particularly fact-specific.

Lay Employees and Church Discipline

The wider issue of the extent to which lay employees can be required to conform to general church discipline has come before the ECtHR five fairly recent cases.[86]

86 The issue of the employment position of ordained ministers also came before the Court in *Hanna and Peter Müller v Germany* [2008] ECHR 12986/04, which involved a claim by two Salvation Army officers for (in effect) unfair dismissal. They had signed a declaration of commitment by which they expressly consented not to be employed by the Army and not to conclude an employment contract with it. The result, however, is inconclusive. The Court rejected their argument under Article 6 §1 that they had not had the opportunity of a proper hearing of their claim. The Court also noted that, except in very exceptional cases, the right to freedom of religion as guaranteed by Article 9 precluded the exercise of any discretion by states parties in assessing the legitimacy of religious beliefs or the means of their expression.

In *Obst*,[87] it was held that the dismissal by the Church of Jesus Christ of Latter-day Saints (LDS) of its Director of Public Relations for Europe on grounds of adultery had not breached Article 8 ECHR (respect for private and family life) because the German labour courts had taken account of all the relevant factors and undertaken a careful and thorough balancing exercise regarding the interests involved. The Court also noted that, having grown up as a Mormon, the claimant had been, or should have been, aware of the importance of marital fidelity for his employer and of the incompatibility of his extramarital relationship with his position in the Church.

In *Schüth*,[88] a Roman Catholic parish and deanery organist and choirmaster left his wife and settled with a new partner with whom he had a child. He was dismissed on the grounds that his functions were so closely connected to the proclamatory mission of the Church that the parish could not continue employing him without losing credibility. The Court held that this had breached his rights under Article 8 ECHR. The German labour courts that had considered his original case had paid no regard to his *de facto* family life with his new partner or to the legal protection afforded it; and while Mr Schüth had entered into a duty of loyalty towards the Church which limited his right to respect for his private life to some degree, his signature on the contract could not be interpreted as an unequivocal commitment to celibacy in the event of separation or divorce.

Obst and *Schüth* were both decided by the Fifth Section and the judgments were handed down on the same day. What seemed to distinguish the two in the minds of the judges were the relative public profiles of the two men: Obst was a national officer of the LDS while Schüth was an obscure church musician. That distinction now seems to be less likely, however, in the light of two more recent cases.

In *Siebenhaar*,[89] the applicant, a Roman Catholic, worked as a childcare assistant in a day nursery run by a Protestant parish in Pforzheim. She was dismissed without notice by the Baden Protestant Church after she became involved with a religious community, the 'Church Universal / Brotherhood of Mankind', whose teachings were deemed by her employer to be incompatible with those of the *Evangelische Kirche in Deutschland* (EKD). The Fifth Section concluded that there had been no breach of Article 9 read in light of Article 11 (freedom of assembly and association): partly because Germany had a system of labour courts whose decisions were reviewable by a constitutional court and

---

87 *Obst v Germany* [2010] ECHR No. 425/03.

88 *Schüth v Germany* [2010] ECHR No. 1620/03.

89 *Siebenhaar v Germany* [2011] ECHR No. 18136/02.

had therefore complied with its positive obligations under the ECHR—and partly because

> the complainant was or should have been aware, when signing her employment contract … that her membership in the Universal Church and her activities in support of it were inconsistent with her commitment to the Protestant Church [46].

In *Fernández Martínez*,[90] the Grand Chamber appeared to tilt the balance still further towards the employer. Mr Fernández Martínez had been ordained a Roman Catholic priest in 1961 but in 1984 had applied for a dispensation from celibacy. He then married in a civil ceremony and from 1991 onwards taught Roman Catholic religion and morals in a state high school, his contract being renewed annually by the local bishop. In 1996 a newspaper published a photograph of him attending a meeting of the Movement for Optional Celibacy with his wife and their five children. In 1997 the Vatican finally dispensed him from celibacy but stated that anyone so dispensed was barred from teaching the Catholic religion in public institutions unless the local bishop decided otherwise according to his own criteria and provided that there was no scandal. In September 1997, his bishop decided not to renew his contract for the new school year.

The majority could see no reason of principle why the notion of 'private life' should be taken to exclude professional activities [110]; and in the case of Mr Martínez, 'the interaction between private life *stricto sensu* and professional life is especially striking' because there was a direct link between his conduct in private life and his professional activities [111]. Moreover, though Mr Martínez had never had a permanent contract, he had a reasonable presumption that his contract would be renewed so long as he was professionally-competent and there were no circumstances that might justify its non-renewal under canon law [112]. Article 8 ECHR was therefore applicable.

Nevertheless, the Grand Chamber dismissed his claim, holding by nine votes to eight that there had been no violation and by fourteen votes to three that there was no need separately to examine his other complaints. The Spanish courts had taken sufficient account of all the relevant factors and had weighed the competing interests in a detailed and comprehensive manner, within the limits imposed by the respect that was due to the autonomy of the Roman Catholic Church [151]. The principle of Church autonomy did not seem to have

90 *Fernández Martínez v Spain* [2014] ECHR 615.

been invoked improperly; and the bishop's decision did not appear to have been insufficiently reasoned, arbitrary or incompatible with the exercise of the Church's autonomy as protected under the Convention [151]. The interference with his right to respect for his private life had been within the margin of appreciation accorded to states parties and had not been disproportionate [152].[91]

It is difficult, to say the least, to derive any consistent principle from the four cases. If Ms Siebenhaar should have known that membership of the Universal Church was incompatible with working for a day-nursery run by the EKD, Mr Obst that the LDS did not look kindly on adultery and Mr Fernández Martínez that the Vatican had firm views about celibacy then, equally, Mr Schüth must have been aware of his Church's disapproval of adulterous relationships—even of stable ones. Moreover, the justification in *Siebenhaar* that the system of labour courts complied with German's obligations under the ECHR does not help us, given that exactly the same system of labour courts was in place in the cases of Mr Obst and Mr Schüth.

The differences between *Obst* and *Schüth* on the one hand and *Siebenhaar* on the other may possibly be these. The first two cases involved a conflict between the right to private and family life under Article 8 ECHR and the religious autonomy of the two Churches in question. In *Siebenhaar*, however, the issue for *both* parties to the dispute was the right to manifest one's religious belief under Article 9: the EKD was claiming the right to organise itself in accordance with its own ecclesiology while Ms Siebenhaar was arguing that her dismissal had breached her right to manifest.

As to the judgment in *Fernández Martínez*, it is difficult to assess its likely future impact, given that it was decided by a single vote—and, in my view, wrongly decided; however, it is consistent with the recent tendency of the Grand Chamber, especially, not to want to get involved in religious disputes if at all possible and to give states parties a very wide margin of appreciation in such matters. Moreover, in the most recent case, *Travaš*,[92] the Court followed *Fernández Martínez*. The applicant had lost his job because his canonical mandate to teach Roman Catholic religion in two State high schools had been withdrawn after he divorced his first wife and remarried in a civil ceremony without first obtaining annulment of his previous marriage. The Court concluded that, given the state's margin of appreciation, the interference with his Article 8 rights was not disproportionate.

Whether or not the Grand Chamber is suffering from an overdose of *Realpolitik* remains an open question; but what all these cases illustrate in their

91 For a full analysis of the judgment, see Cranmer (2014).

92 *Travaš v Croatia* [2016] ECHR 813: for a discussion see Strauss (2016).

different ways is this: *Churches and other religious organisation, as employers, need to be exceedingly careful about the way in which they deal with lay employees*. The facts of the individual case are absolutely crucial, as is the importance of having in place a fair and transparent disciplinary procedure. Nor is it necessarily the case that the standards of doctrinal orthodoxy or of personal behaviour that are expected of clergy can simply be imposed on the laity.

Church-Workers and Trades Union Membership

The right of workers to join a union—and, by implication, the right of church workers to do so—was recognised in the social teaching of the Roman Catholic Church over fifty years ago by the Second Vatican Council in *Gaudium et Spes* (Montini: 1965, 68):

> Among the basic rights of the human person is to be numbered the right of freely founding unions for working people. These should be able truly to represent them and to contribute to the organizing of economic life in the right way. Included is the right of freely taking part in the activity of these unions without risk of reprisal.[93]

As to the domestic situation, Unite the Union has a faith organisations branch that includes two denominational sub-groups: Church of England Clergy Advocates and the Association of Methodist Faith Workers, which is open to all who work for the Methodist Church, whether ordained or lay (Unite: 2017).

Strasbourg, however, appears to be prepared to give states parties a very wide margin of appreciation in the matter. In *Sindicatul Păstorul Cel Bun*,[94] clergy and lay employees of the Romanian Orthodox Church established the Union of the Good Shepherd with the aim, as set out in its statutes, of defending the professional, economic, social and cultural interests of its members in their dealings with the Church hierarchy and the Ministry of Cultural and Religious Affairs. However, after objections from the Church the Romanian authorities refused to register the union.

The union took its case to Strasbourg, arguing that the refusal had infringed its rights under Article 11 ECHR (freedom of assembly and association) and that the reasons given by the domestic court to justify the interference by the

93 *Inter fundamentalia personae humanae iura adnumerandum est ius pro laborantibus consociationes libere condendi, quae eos vere repraesentare et ad vitam oeconomicam recto ordine disponendam conferre possint, necnon ius earum navitatem sine ultionis periculo libere participandi.*

94 *Sindicatul Păstorul Cel Bun v Romania* [2012] ECHR 2330/09.

authorities had been of a purely religious nature: it had not examined the repercussions of the employment contract on the employer-employee relationship, the distinction between members of the clergy and lay employees of the Church or the issue as to whether or not the ecclesiastical rules prohibiting union membership were compatible with the domestic and international regulations giving employees the right to belong to a union. The Orthodox Church argued that it was a matter of canon law and claimed the protection of Article 9. Following *Schüth*, the Third Section concluded that

> the relationship based on an employment contract cannot be 'clericalised' to the point of escaping any rule of civil law ... [and] that the clergy and, even more so, lay employees of the Church cannot be removed from the scope of Article 11. National authorities may at most impose 'lawful restrictions' in accordance with Article 11§2 of the Convention [65].

So, in the absence of a 'pressing social need' or of sufficient reasons for the restriction, the Third Section held by five votes to two that there had indeed been a violation of Article 11.

Romania then appealed to the Grand Chamber, which reversed the Third Section, holding by eleven votes to six that there had been no violation of Article 11.[95] Religious communities 'traditionally and universally exist in the form of organised structures' [136] and, so far as the question of organisation was at issue, Article 9 had to be interpreted in light of Article 11:

> Seen from this perspective, the right of believers to freedom of religion encompasses the expectation that the community will be allowed to function peacefully, free from arbitrary State intervention. The autonomous existence of religious communities is indispensable for pluralism in a democratic society and is an issue at the very heart of the protection which Article 9 affords [136].

The majority agreed that the refusal to register the applicant union interfered with the Article 11 rights of its members [149] but concluded that the interference was prescribed by law, pursued a legitimate aim and was necessary in a democratic society. In short:

> Having regard to the lack of a European consensus on this matter ... the State enjoys a wider margin of appreciation in this sphere, encompassing

95 *Sindicatul Păstorul Cel Bun v Romania* [2013] ECHR 646.

> the right to decide whether or not to recognise trade unions that operate within religious communities and pursue aims that might hinder the exercise of such communities' autonomy [171].

Employment and the Religious Exception

The Religious Exception

Schedule 9 to the Equality Act 2010 provides two exceptions for employment: 9(2) provides a separate exception from laws prohibiting discrimination on grounds of sex, marriage and sexual orientation and 9(3) allows employers with an ethos based on religion or belief to discriminate on those grounds. In addition, 9(2) applies where three criteria are met.

First, the employment must be for the purposes of an organised religion—and in *R (Amicus MSF Section)*,[96] Richards J held that term 'organised religion' was narrower than 'religious organisation', suggesting that employment as a teacher in a faith school was likely to be 'for purposes of a religious organisation' but not 'for purposes of an organised religion' [116]. The Explanatory Notes to the Act state at paragraph 799 that this is 'intended to cover a very narrow range of employment: ministers of religion and a small number of lay posts, including those that exist to promote and represent religion'. How much reliance can be placed on Explanatory Notes is arguable, given that they are not part of the Act, but there is always the possibility that they might be cited in case of dispute.

Secondly, the Act specifies in Schedule 9 2(5) that the discrimination must be 'so as to comply with the doctrines of the religion'[97] and the purpose of the discrimination must be 'to avoid conflicting with the strongly held convictions of a significant number of the religion's followers'. In *R (Amicus MSF Section)* Richards J stated that that those requirements imposed 'very real additional limitations' [117] and suggested that both tests were objective. But it is not clear precisely how that objectivity could be brought to bear in any specific case. In the opinion of Richards J:

> As to the expression 'a significant number', that is an ordinary English expression which courts or tribunals should have no difficulty in applying in practice: cf. 'considerably smaller' in other discrimination legislation, which has proved workable in practice [107].

96 *R (Amicus MSF Section) v Secretary of State for Trade and Industry* [2004] EWHC 860.

97 Equality Act 2010, Schedule 9 Para 2(5).

But be that as it may, it remains the case that different people will have different views as to what constitutes the 'significant number' who have to be offended in order to engage the exception. As to what constitutes 'the religion's followers', different denominations have very different criteria for membership. The Church of England, for example, teaches that membership is conferred through baptism; however, the terms of the Equality Act would suggest that, in deciding whether to apply a requirement, regard should be had to the convictions of *the worshipping members* of the Church.[98] So does that mean those who are on the electoral role, or does it include those who only ever go to church at Christmas? And how do you find out whether or not the worshipping members *are*, in fact, offended?

Thirdly, the employer can discriminate either where the employee does not meet the requirement imposed or where the employer is not satisfied *and it is reasonable for him not to be satisfied that that person meets it.*

The importance of this reasonableness requirement was stressed in *Reaney*.[99] Mr Reaney, who applied for the post of Diocesan Youth Officer, had been in a committed same-sex relationship that had ended prior to his application. He was turned down for the post after the Bishop had expressed his concern about his previous relationship, had asked for further reassurances about his future lifestyle and had then refused to accept his assurance that he would remain celibate. The Bishop concluded that he could not promise not to have a same-sex relationship in future and did not, therefore, offer him the post. Mr Reaney took the matter to an Employment Tribunal, claiming harassment and discrimination on the grounds of sexual orientation contrary to the Employment Equality (Sexual Orientation) Regulations 2003.

The Tribunal rejected the claim of harassment [92]; but on the issue of discrimination concluded that the Regulations did not make a distinction between the mere fact of being gay and expressing that sexual orientation in behaviour and accepted Mr Reaney's submission that the Regulations had to be read consistently with his Convention rights [97]. The Tribunal held that although employment as a Diocesan Youth Officer was 'for the purposes of an organised religion' [100–102] and the Bishop had been permitted to apply a requirement related to sexual orientation on either of the grounds set out in the Regulations [103–104], the religious exception did not apply because Mr Reaney *did* meet the requirement imposed and it was unreasonable for the Bishop to have concluded otherwise [106].

---

98 (2017a) [emphasis added].

99 *Reaney v Hereford Diocesan Board of Finance* [2007] ET 1602844/2006.

The Definition of 'Philosophical Belief'

As noted above, the exception in Schedule 9(3) to the Equality Act 2010 applies as much to employers with an ethos based on 'belief' as to employers with an ethos based on 'religion', while s.10 of that Act defines the protected characteristic of religion or belief as follows:

(1) Religion means any religion and a reference to religion includes a reference to a lack of religion.
(2) Belief means any religious or philosophical belief and a reference to belief includes a reference to a lack of belief.
(3) In relation to the protected characteristic of religion or belief—
   (a) a reference to a person who has a particular protected characteristic is a reference to a person of a particular religion or belief;
   (b) a reference to persons who share a protected characteristic is a reference to persons who are of the same religion or belief.

The Employment Equality (Religion or Belief) Regulations 2003 were drafted in more general terms, Regulation 2(1) stating that 'In these Regulations, "religion or belief" means any religion, religious belief, or similar philosophical belief'. In *Grainger*,[100] Burton J set out at [24] the limits to be placed upon the definition of 'philosophical belief' for the purpose of the 2003 Regulations as follows:

(i) The belief must be genuinely held.
(ii) It must be a belief and not ... an opinion or viewpoint based on the present state of information available.
(iii) It must be a belief as to a weighty and substantial aspect of human life and behaviour.
(iv) It must attain a certain level of cogency, seriousness, cohesion and importance.[101]
(v) It must be worthy of respect in a democratic society, be not incompatible with human dignity and not conflict with the fundamental rights of others.

100 *Grainger Plc & Ors v Nicholson* [2009] UKEAT 0219/09/0311.

101 Echoing the statement in *Campbell and Cosans v United Kingdom* [1982] ECHR 1 that in its ordinary meaning the word 'convictions', taken on its own, was not synonymous with the words 'opinions' and 'ideas': it was more akin to the term 'beliefs' in Article 9 '*and denotes views that attain a certain level of cogency, seriousness, cohesion and importance*' [36: emphasis added].

He added at [26] that 'it is necessary, in order for the belief to be protected, for it to have a similar status or cogency to a religious belief'.

The criteria in *Grainger* have been followed subsequently. In *Brown*,[102] for example, Cox J rejected the claimant's contention that living on a boat constituted a religious or philosophical belief within the meaning of s.10(2) of the Equality Act 102:

> For a philosophical belief to be protected it must be 'a belief as to a weighty and substantial aspect of human life and behaviour' and must 'attain a certain level of cogency, seriousness, cohesion and importance', see *Nicholson v Grainger plc* [2010] ICR 360. As Mr Justice Burton added at paragraph 26 in that case, 'it is necessary, in order for the belief to be protected, for it to have a similar status or cogency to a religious belief', in contrast to a mere 'lifestyle choice'.

The Genuine Occupational Requirement

The Employment Equality (Religion or Belief) Regulations 2003 provided an exception in relation to discrimination on grounds of religion or belief where, 'having regard to the nature of the employment or the context in which it is carried out', being of a particular religion or belief was a 'genuine and determining occupational requirement' and it was proportionate to apply that requirement in the particular case. The Genuine Occupational Requirement ('GOR') exception is restated in paragraph 3 of schedule 9 to the Equality Act 2010; and once the claimant has established that he or she has suffered a disadvantage on grounds of religion, the burden of proof shifts to the employer to show that the occupational requirement complained of can be justified.

What is—and what is not—a GOR has inevitably given rise to dispute.[103] In the linked cases of *Hender*[104] and *Sheridan*,[105] the claimants were employed by Prospects, which provided housing and day-care for people with learning disabilities. Prospects was both a charity and a company limited by guarantee and it was founded with an overtly-Christian ethos: its memorandum and articles of association included at clause 3(m) a statement of faith in, *inter alia*, the inerrancy of the Bible as the inspired word of God, the Trinity, the virgin conception of Jesus, his death 'in the place of sinners' and his resurrection and

102 *R (Brown) v Canal River Trust* [2012] EWHC 3133 (Admin).

103 The Advisory Conciliation and Arbitration Service (2014, Appendix I) has helpful guidance on the Genuine Occupational Requirement.

104 *Hender v Prospects for People with Learning Disabilities* [2008] ET 2902090/2006.

105 *Sheridan v Prospects for People with Learning Disabilities* [2008] ET 2901366/2006.

ascension [*Hender* 2.3]. The charity's policy was to recruit Christian staff wherever possible; failing that, non-Christians were obliged to sign a form acknowledging their sympathy with its aims and beliefs and agreeing to work within its policies [*Hender* 2.4].

After the Employment Equality (Religion or Belief) Regulations 2003 had come into force, the Chief Executive sent a memorandum to senior management pointing out that it was illegal to advertise for Christian staff unless Prospects could demonstrate a GOR for its posts [*Hender* 2.5]. By February 2005, Prospects had told its staff that all roles except cooking, cleaning, gardening, maintenance and relief staff were now subject to Christian profession as a GOR because those in post might have to lead prayers or give spiritual guidance [*Hender* 2.19]. The charity advised non-Christian employees that they could remain in post; however, it was later decided that only practising Christians could be recruited or promoted to Level 2 posts [*Hender* 2.19 & 2.20].

Mrs Hender was refused promotion, while Mr Sheridan resigned because he was unhappy with the policy that he was obliged to operate—and he wrote to the Chief Executive telling him so. Prospects did not carry out a job evaluation for every vacant post; instead, it made a decision in principle that all posts should be filled by Christians and assumed that that was sufficient to comply with the 2003 Regulations—an approach that proved to be fatally flawed when the Employment Tribunal concluded that Mr Sheridan had been constructively dismissed and Mrs Hender had been denied promotion on improper grounds. In short, in order to be beyond challenge *a Genuine Occupational Requirement has to be genuine.*

But, that said, 'genuineness' is decided on the facts. In *Muhammed*,[106] the Leprosy Mission, a Christian charity, refused an application from a Muslim for a vacancy as a finance administrator. The Employment Tribunal held that the Mission could legitimately refuse applications from non-Christians because Christianity permeated the organisation: for example, each day started with prayers. Employing a non-Christian would have had a significant impact on the ability of the organisation to maintain its ethos, whereas the applicant who had been refused the job would have the chance to work elsewhere.

Finally, in order to apply a GOR, the employing organisation must be able to demonstrate that it has a religious or philosophical ethos that merits respect. In *McNab*,[107] the primary issue before the EAT was whether or not it was a GOR for a particular teaching post that the holder should be a practising

106 *Muhammed v Leprosy Mission International* [2009] ET 2303459/09.

107 *Glasgow City Council v McNab* [2007] UKEAT 0037 06 1701. For a discussion of the more general issues of employment in faith schools see Vickers (2009).

Roman Catholic. The claimant, an atheist who was teaching in a Roman Catholic school, applied for a post within the school as a pastoral care teacher but was not offered an interview. Glasgow City Council, which maintained the school, had assumed that the Church would have regarded profession of the Roman Catholic faith as a prerequisite for the post; the Employment Tribunal, however, concluded that the responsibilities of the post involved giving advice on a large number of issues; only a few of them required knowledge of Roman Catholic doctrine and those particular issues could be handled by a different teacher [20]. The EAT agreed that it was not a 'genuine and determining' requirement in terms of Regulation 7(2) of the Employment Equality (Religion or Belief) Regulations 2003 that the post be held by a Roman Catholic. In addition, however, the EAT held that Glasgow City Council 'were not entitled to have recourse to regulation 7(3) as they could not show that they were an employer who had "an ethos based on religion or belief"' [61].

What if Religious Views are in Conflict?

In *G v P*,[108] Ms P worked as a donor processor for a faith-based charity whose fundraising arm produced and broadcast Christian television programmes. The donor processors were required to perform two key functions: to receive calls from the public and discuss the spiritual and theological content of the organisation's broadcasts and to process donations from viewers and supporters.

The organisation took the view that, in order to be able to discuss the content of the broadcasts, the donor processors needed to have a detailed understanding of the specific tenets of its faith as well as a strong grasp of Scripture. The job also had a pastoral element: donor processors often had to speak to vulnerable people or those seeking guidance or consolation. The organisation therefore ran structured prayer and training sessions to help prepare them for their role and ensure that standards were upheld. But Ms P refused to participate in the sessions, arguing that her own beliefs and her own interpretations of Scripture derived from her direct relationship with God and that any attempt to establish a uniform understanding through structured training and prayer constituted an interference with that direct relationship. She was given two opportunities to change her mind, following which her contract was terminated on notice.

The ET concluded at a pre-hearing review that the organisation had not treated P less favourably because of her—or its own—Christian beliefs. Both parties shared precisely the same set of beliefs: Ms P's contract had been

108 *G v P* [2013] Ashford Employment Tribunal (unreported). The Tribunal delivered an oral decision only: this is based, with permission, on a report by Paul Jennings (2013, 12).

terminated because she had refused to participate in the structured training. Her allegation of direct religious discrimination was therefore struck out in advance of the full hearing. At the substantive hearing on the unfair dismissal claim, the Tribunal concluded that it had been legitimate and reasonable for the organisation to want uniformity in its communications with its supporters; if donor processors were left to communicate with the public on complex theological issues without any training or control over standards it would expose the organisation to a genuine risk. The organisation had therefore acted entirely reasonably in the circumstances—and the claim was dismissed.

The Right to Manifest Religion in the Workplace and Conscientious Objection

Issues of manifestation in the workplace over matters such as conscientious objection, work patterns and religious dress have come before the courts time and time again and, as we shall see, the ground appears to be shifting—very slowly—away from the employer.

Copsey *and Sunday Working*

In *Copsey*,[109] the claimant worked as a team leader in the sand processing operations of WWB Devon Clays Ltd from March 1988 to July 2002. He worked shifts from Monday to Friday, with frequent overtime on Saturdays and occasional overtime on Sundays. In late 1999 Devon Clays won a new order requiring a substantial increase in production and decided that the only way to fulfil it was to extend the operating hours to 7-day 24-hour working with 12-hour shifts. Mr Copsey refused to work Sundays on religious grounds and was dismissed.

Though it was argued that Article 9 ECHR was engaged, both the ET and the EAT held that he was dismissed for 'some other substantial reason' falling within section 98(1)(b) of the Employment Rights Act 1996 [17, 19]. The alternatives to dismissal had been fully explored with Mr Copsey and the ET had found that Devon Clays had done everything possible to accommodate his requirement not to work on any Sundays.

The initial accommodation had been successful, but it then led to difficulties, not least because of dissatisfaction among other employees. Devon Clays then offered him an arrangement which would have minimised his Sunday working, and, subsequently, a new (admittedly less well-paid) post that would have avoided any Sunday working at all [95]. But he refused; and no sensible

109 *Copsey v WBB Devon Clays Ltd* [2005] EWCA Civ 932.

alternative to dismissal could be found. In those circumstances, the Court of Appeal held that the Employment Tribunal had been entitled to conclude that the dismissal was justified and his appeal was dismissed unanimously.

Eweida *and Its Possible Consequences*

Copsey was a somewhat isolated case, but several subsequent judgments have returned to issues of manifestation, probably the most important of which is *Eweida*.[110]

Eweida consisted of four conjoined appeals from the UK courts involving four separate claimants who argued, as committed Christians, that the actions of their employers had violated their rights in various respects to manifest their religion under Article 9: Nadia Eweida (a check-in clerk with BA plc, formerly known as British Airways), Shirley Chaplin (a nursing sister), Lillian Ladele (a local authority registrar) and Gary McFarlane (a relationships counsellor with Relate Avon Ltd).

Ms Eweida wished to wear a cross and chain around her neck, in contravention of BA's uniform code. Mrs Chaplin had been told by her NHS Trust that she was not permitted, on health and safety grounds, to wear the crucifix that she had worn on a neck-chain since her confirmation as a member of the Free Church of England. Ms Ladele, a registrar of births, deaths and marriages with the London Borough of Islington from 2002 onwards, was told in 2005 that Islington had decided to designate all existing registrars of births, deaths and marriages as civil partnership registrars and when she refused on grounds of conscience to conduct civil partnerships she was dismissed. Mr McFarlane had told his employers that, though he was prepared to counsel same-sex couples and in fact did so, he had conscientious scruples about giving them psychosexual counselling in spite of having volunteered for Relate's post-graduate diploma in psychosexual therapy—and he was ultimately dismissed.

Ms Eweida won, the other three lost. In brief, the Court decided:

- (by five votes to two) that the refusal by BA between September 2006 and February 2007 to allow Ms Eweida to remain in her post while wearing a visible cross with her uniform amounted to an interference with her right to manifest her religion under Article 9, that BA's actions had been disproportionate and that the Court of Appeal had not struck the correct balance in its ruling in favour of BA and that 'while [BA's] aim was undoubtedly legitimate, the domestic courts accorded it too much weight' [94];

---

110 *Eweida and Others v United Kingdom* [2013] ECHR 37.

- (unanimously) that Ms Chaplin's freedom to manifest her religion by wearing her crucifix on a neck-chain had been interfered with but that the interference had been legitimate—she had been offered the alternative of wearing her crucifix under a high-necked top beneath her tunic or attached to the lanyard that held her security pass but had not regarded either as a satisfactory accommodation—and that because the ban was on grounds of health and safety in a hospital ward it was inherently of greater magnitude than BA's uniform policy, which was about corporate image [99];
- (by five votes to two) that though the Court agreed with Ms Ladele that the local authority's requirement that all registrars be designated to conduct civil partnerships had been particularly detrimental to her because of her religious beliefs, the authority's policy was aimed at securing the rights of others that were also protected under the Convention and had not exceeded the margin of appreciation available to it [106]; and
- (unanimously) that Mr McFarlane had enrolled voluntarily on Relate Avon's training programme in psychosexual counselling knowing that Relate operated an Equal Opportunities Policy and that he would not be able to refuse psychosexual counselling to same-sex couples, that Relate's action in dismissing him when he *did*, in fact, refuse was intended to secure the implementation of its policy of providing a service without discrimination and that, in all the circumstances, the margin of appreciation had not been exceeded [109].

Crucially for what follows, the Court observed that

> In order to count as a 'manifestation' within the meaning of Article 9, the act in question must be intimately linked to the religion or belief. An example would be an act of worship or devotion which forms part of the practice of a religion or belief in a generally recognised form. However, the manifestation of religion or belief is not limited to such acts; the existence of a sufficiently close and direct nexus between the act and the underlying belief must be determined on the facts of each case. In particular, *there is no requirement on the applicant to establish that he or she acted in fulfilment of a duty mandated by the religion in question* [82: emphasis added].

Mark Hill (2013) suggests that the judgment in *Eweida* has various consequences for domestic courts. First, it made clear that they should not assess the legitimacy of religious beliefs or the ways in which those beliefs are expressed: provided the claimed beliefs and their expression attained the required level of cogency, seriousness, cohesion and importance, there was to be no examination of their veracity. Secondly, it declared that was unnecessary for a belief to be doctrinally mandated in order for its manifestation to be protected under Article 9: prior to the judgment, domestic law had protected the right of Sikhs to wear the *kara* bangle and the *kirpan* ritual dagger but not the right of Christians to wear a cross. Thirdly, the judgment

> has made it plain that where an individual complains of a restriction on freedom of religion in the workplace, it is not enough to assert that the possibility of changing job will negate any interference with the right to freedom of religion. Employers will no longer be able to say: we are not stopping any employee practising their religion because he or she can simply resign and move to another job.

In short, Hill suggests that *Eweida* signalled the end of the 'specific situation rule' enunciated in *Kalaç*[111]—otherwise, 'like it or leg it'—but how long it will be before the third of these becomes embedded in domestic law and practice remains to be seen. My suspicion is that it might be rather a slow process.

Religious Dress

The issue of religious dress—and not just in the workplace—has been a major issue in discussions of religion and employment law, both domestically and under the ECHR. In the wider context, the decision of the Grand Chamber of the ECtHR in *S.A.S.*[112] upholding the French ban on covering the face in public attracted criticism right across the religious spectrum, from devout Muslims to

111 *Kalaç v Turkey* [1997] ECHR 37, in which the compulsory retirement of the Director of Legal Affairs of the Turkish Air Force for having adopted 'unlawful fundamentalist opinions' was held not to have violated Article 9. The Court held that military service involved accepting military discipline that might restrict the rights and freedoms of personnel in ways that could not be imposed on civilians. Within those constraints, Group Captain Kalaç had been able to fulfil his religious obligations such as prayer five times a day, keeping Ramadan and attending Friday prayers at the mosque. He had been retired not been because of his religious opinions and beliefs but because his conduct and attitude had breached military discipline and infringed the principle of secularism. Crucially, declared the Court, Article 9 did not protect every act motivated or inspired by a religion or belief and '*in exercising his freedom to manifest his religion, an individual may need to take his specific situation into account*' [27: emphasis added].

112 *S.A.S. v France* [2014] ECHR 695.

confirmed secularists[113]—but that ban was a general one under France's Law of 11 October 2010 'prohibiting the concealment of one's face in public places'. The judgment in *S.A.S* was followed recently in two Belgian cases involving bans on the *niqab*: *Belcacemi* and *Dakir*;[114] in both, the Court was prepared to grant a wide margin of appreciation to the Belgian Government, given that there was still no consensus among the membership of the Council of Europe about its acceptability. And turning specifically to the workplace, the position on religious dress after *Eweida* still seems somewhat unclear.

In *Ebrahimian*,[115] Nanterre Hospital refused to renew the contract of a psychiatric social worker unless she stopped wearing a *hijab*[116] after some patients complained. The Court held by six votes to one that there had been no violation of Article 9. Her *hijab* was an ostentatious manifestation of her religion and incompatible with the neutral space required by a public service [62]; and it was clear from the record that the contested decision was founded on the

113 Lucy Vickers, for example, points out (2014) that the judgment builds a strong case that banning the *burqa* in public would breach human rights standards, would be alien to European values, would be contrary to the 'almost universal' consensus in other European states against bans in public spaces, would be unnecessary in order to achieve most of the legitimate aims that have been used previously to justify bans on religious symbols and is not necessary to ensure public safety—*then goes on completely to ignore the case against the ban that it has so carefully constructed.* She concludes that the ban 'is not necessary to uphold gender equality; nor is it necessary for human dignity'.

114 *Belcacemi and Oussar v Belgium* [2017] ECHR 655 and *Dakir v Belgium* [2017] ECHR 656. The first challenged the national law of 1 June 2011 banning the wearing in public places of clothing which partially or totally covers the face and the second challenged a by-law adopted in June 2008 by the municipalities of Pepinster, Dison and Verviers providing in Article 113*bis* for a similar local ban. The claimants, between them, alleged violations of Articles 3, 5 §1, 8, 9, 10, 11 and Article 2 of Protocol No 4 taken separately and together with Article 14—but the Court held that none of those Articles had been violated. Ms Dakir, however, also relied on Article 6 §1, claiming that the *Conseil d'État* had not examined her arguments on their merits on the grounds that she had not directed her action against Article 113 of the by-law when, in reality, she had properly directed it against Article 113*bis* which, according to the *Conseil* itself, was a repetition. The Court agreed with her that the *Conseil's* admissibility conditions for her application had been excessively rigid and held that, in her case, there had been a violation of the right under Article 6 §1 to a fair and public hearing within a reasonable time: (Cranmer, 2017).

115 *Ebrahimian v France* [2015] ECHR 1041.

116 The French text of the majority describes her as wearing a *voile*, but the partially concurring and partially dissenting judgment of O'Leary J and the dissenting judgment of De Gaetano J—both in English—make clear that Ms Ebrahimian had been wearing a *hijab* to work rather than a *niqab*.

imperative of protecting the rights and freedom of others, not on the claimant's religious beliefs [63]. In a public hospital, patients should not be in doubt about the impartiality of the staff [64]. The interference was therefore proportionate to the aim pursued and, in the circumstances, a wide margin of appreciation was appropriate [65].

The majority judgment attracted a withering dissent from De Gaetano J in a very short opinion:

> The judgment proceeds from and rests on the false (and, I would add, very dangerous) premise … that the users of public services cannot be guaranteed an impartial service if the public official serving them manifests in the slightest way his or her religious affiliation—even though quite often, from the very name of the official displayed on the desk or elsewhere, one can be reasonably certain of the religious affiliation of that official.[117]
>
> Moreover, it would also seem that what is prohibited under French law with regard to public officials is the *subjective* manifestation of one's religious belief and not the *objective* wearing of a particular piece of clothing or other symbol. A woman may wear a headscarf not to manifest a religious belief, or any belief for that matter, but for a variety of other reasons. The same can be said of a man wearing a full beard, or a person wearing a cross with a necklace. Requiring a public official to 'disclose' whether that item of clothing is a manifestation or otherwise of his or her religious belief does not sit well with the purported benefits enjoyed by public officials as mentioned in paragraph 66 of the judgment.
>
> While States have a wide margin of appreciation as to the conditions of service of public officials, that margin is not without limits. A principle of constitutional law or a constitutional 'tradition' may easily end up by being deified, thereby undermining every value underpinning the Convention. This judgment comes dangerously close to doing exactly that.

At about the same time, an Employment Tribunal held in *Begum*[118] that there had been no discrimination against an observant Muslim refused a job as a trainee nursery assistant because she believed that her religion required her to wear a *jilbab* dress/coat reaching from her neck to her ankles, while the company

117 Although it should be said that 'Christiane' seems a slightly unusual first name for a Muslim.

118 *Begum v Pedagogy Auras UK Ltd (t/a Barley Lane Montessori Day Nursery)* [2015] UKEAT 0309/13/2205.

had a rule that staff should not wear any garment that might constitute a tripping hazard to themselves or to the children in their care. But that case was as much about health and safety as about the right to manifest: the possibility of an unfortunate accident outweighed Ms Begum's religious sensibilities.

Achbita, Bougnaoui *and the* ECJ

Most recently, the issue came before the European Court of Justice in two cases decided by the Grand Chamber on the same day: *G4S Secure Solutions*[119]—more commonly known as *Achbita*—and *Bougnaoui*.[120] They were the first two judgments by the Court on discrimination on grounds of religion or belief since the adoption of the Framework Directive on equal treatment in employment and occupation—and both involved *hijabs* at work.

Samira Achbita, a Muslim, worked as a receptionist for G4S and after three years insisted that she should be allowed to wear a *hijab*. G4S prohibits employees from wearing any visible religious, political or philosophical symbols and, consequently, dismissed her. The Belgian *Cour de Cassation/Hof van Cassatie* asked the ECJ for a preliminary ruling as to whether Article 2(2)(a) the Framework Directive should be interpreted as meaning that prohibiting a female Muslim from wearing a headscarf at work was not direct discrimination where the employer's rule prohibited all employees from wearing outward signs of political, philosophical and religious beliefs in the workplace.

In the opinion of Advocate General Kokott,[121] the facts had not revealed any direct religious discrimination, always provided that the ban had been based on a general company rule prohibiting visible political, philosophical and religious symbols rather than on religious stereotypes or prejudices. In her view, the ban might constitute *indirect* religious discrimination but could be justified if it enforced G4S's legitimate policy of religious and ideological neutrality, taking into account the size and conspicuousness of the religious symbol, the nature of the Ms Achbita's activity, the context in which she had to work and 'the national identity of the Member State concerned'. It was for the Belgian Court to strike a fair balance between the conflicting interests. She also observed that

> unlike sex, skin colour, ethnic origin, sexual orientation, age or a person's disability, the practice of religion is not so much an unalterable fact as an aspect of an individual's private life, and one, moreover, over which

119 *G4S Secure Solutions NV* [2017] EUECJ C-157/15.

120 *Bougnaoui and ADDH* [2017] EUECJ C-188/15.

121 *Samira Achbita & Anor v G4S Secure Solutions NV* [2016] EUECJ C-157/15.

> the employees concerned can choose to exert an influence. While an employee cannot 'leave' his sex, skin colour, ethnicity, sexual orientation, age or disability 'at the door' upon entering his employer's premises, he may be expected to moderate the exercise of his religion in the workplace, be this in relation to religious practices, religiously motivated behaviour or (as in the present case) his clothing [116].

Asma Bougnaoui, also a Muslim, was a design engineer with Micropole SA, working for its clients on-site. A client told Micropole that her *hijab* had upset a number of its employees and asked that there should be 'no veil next time'. When she refused to stop wearing it, she was dismissed. The French *Cour de Cassation* sought a ruling on whether a customer's wish no longer to have a company's services provided by an employee in a *hijab* was a genuine and determining occupational requirement under Article 4(1) of the Directive 'by reason of the nature of the particular occupational activities concerned or of the context in which they are carried out'.

AG Sharpston took a rather different line in her opinion[122] from AG Kokott's in *Achbita*—though it should be noted that the questions asked by the two courts were slightly different and referred to different Articles of the Directive. AG Sharpston could find no basis on which Article 4(1) could apply to Ms Bougnaoui's work for Micropole. There was nothing to suggest that her *hijab* interfered in any way with her duties as a design engineer; therefore, the requirement not to wear it when in contact with Micropole's customers could not be a 'genuine and determining occupational requirement' [102]. Moreover:

> The pernicious nature of the argument, 'because our employee X is wearing an Islamic headscarf' (or a *kippah*, or a *dastar*) (or is black, homosexual or a woman) 'it follows that (s)he cannot be behaving appropriately towards our clients' should require no further elaboration [74].

The Grand Chamber finessed the issue. In *Achbita*, it ruled that Article 2(2)(a) of Council Directive 2000/78/EC had to be interpreted as meaning that a prohibition on wearing an Islamic headscarf under an internal rule of a private undertaking prohibiting the visible wearing of any political, philosophical or religious sign in the workplace was not direct discrimination based on religion or belief within the meaning of that Directive. It might, however, constitute *indirect* discrimination within the meaning of Article 2(2)(b) if it was established

122 *Asma Bougnaoui and l'Association de défense des droits de l'homme* (ADDH) *v Micropole SA* [2016] EUECJ C188/15.

that the apparently neutral obligation put persons adhering to a particular religion or belief at a particular disadvantage unless it was objectively justified by a legitimate aim, such as the pursuit by the employer of a policy of political, philosophical and religious neutrality in its relations with its customers and provided the means of achieving that aim were appropriate and necessary—which was a matter for the referring court to ascertain [45]. In *Bougnaoui*, it ruled that Article 4(1) had to be interpreted as meaning that the willingness of an employer to take account of the wishes of a customer no longer to have the employer's services provided by a worker wearing a *hijab* was not a genuine and determining occupational requirement within the meaning of the Article [42].

Achbita, Bougnaoui *and the UK Government's Response*

On the day following the two judgments, the Parliamentary Under-Secretary of State for Women and Equalities, Caroline Dinenage, answered an Urgent Question in the Commons from Maria Miller (Basingstoke) (Con), 'if she will make a statement on the recent Court of Justice of the European Union ruling allowing employers to ban workers from wearing religious dress and symbols in the workplace'. In short:

> The Government are completely opposed to discrimination, including on grounds of gender or religion, or both. It is the right of all women to choose how they dress, and we do not believe that the judgments change that. Exactly the same legal protections apply today as applied before the rulings. In both the *Achbita* case and the *Bougnaoui* case, the judgment was that there was no direct discrimination, but that there was some discrimination. A rule is directly discriminatory if it treats someone less favourably because of their sex, race, religion or whatever. A rule is indirectly discriminatory if, on the face of it, it treats everyone the same, but some people, because of their race, religion, sex and so on, find it harder to comply than others do. Indirect discrimination may be justifiable if an employer is acting in a proportionate manner to achieve a legitimate aim.
>
> The judgments confirm the existing long-standing position of EU and domestic law that an employer's dress code, where it applies to and is applied in the same way to all employees, may be justifiable if the employer can show legitimate and proportionate grounds for it. Various cases show that such an employer needs to be prepared to justify those grounds in front of a court or tribunal if need be. That will remain the case and that

> is the case with these judgments, which will now revert to the domestic courts.[123]

She added that the Government would be working with the Equality and Human Rights Commission to update guidance for employers on dealing with religion or belief in the workplace, revised to take account of the two judgments.

The immediate media reaction varied from the measured to the mildly-hysterical. Perhaps the most balanced comment was from Amy Wren (2017):

> where does this leave employers in the UK? Actually, not far from the advice I would usually give in these sort of situations: unless it can clearly be shown that the wearing of religious items is genuinely interfering with employees' ability to carry out work safely and properly, then just don't go there.

Which seems like sound advice. Vickers (2016, 203) concludes that when dealing with disputes about religious symbols and religious dress the courts have adopted a very fact-specific approach 'and it can be difficult to determine in advance whether particular restrictions on religious dress will be justified or not when they cause disadvantage'. Given that uncertainty, therefore, an employer needs to think very hard indeed before telling an employee that she may not wear a *hijab* to work—or even that a minister of religion in secular employment may not wear a clerical shirt and collar.

Mba and Sunday Working

Ms Celestina Mba, a care worker in a local authority children's home, had to work occasional Sundays but, as a practising Christian who took the Fourth Commandment very seriously, she did not wish to do so. In the end, she resigned and claimed unfair dismissal. In *Mba*,[124] the EAT concluded that Merton Borough Council had not discriminated against her on grounds of religion or belief. On further appeal, the EAT judgment was upheld.[125] She argued that Merton could have accommodated her religious convictions about not working on Sundays without affecting the running of the children's home: in short, reasonable accommodation—about which more below.

123 HC Deb (2016–17) 15 March 2017 c 409.

124 *Mba v London Borough of Merton* [2012] UKEAT 0332/12/1312.

125 *Mba v London Borough of Merton* [2013] EWCA Civ 1562.

The Court held that she had not been constructively dismissed. Maurice Kay LJ held that there had been an error of law in the decisions of the lower tribunals [20] but nevertheless concluded that

> the requirements made of Mrs Mba to work on certain Sundays were a proportionate means of achieving an indisputably legitimate aim … once Mrs Mba failed to establish the more favourable terms of the contract for which she had contended and the Council had established that there was really no viable or practicable alternative way of running Brightwell [children's home] effectively, there was only ever going to be one outcome to this case [24].

Permission to appeal to the Supreme Court was refused.

The importance of *Mba* is twofold. First, it revisited the Sunday working issue for the first time since *Copsey*. Secondly—and possibly more important—even though Ms Mba lost her appeal, in line with *Eweida & Ors* the judgment appears to weaken slightly the idea of a simple checklist of 'core beliefs' against which a claim must be assessed: in short, that just because other devout Christians are happy to work on Sundays, that does not mean that someone with a principled religious objection to Sunday working is to be regarded as a religious eccentric. Moreover, Elias LJ referred to justification being read compatibly with Article 9 where that provision was in play:

> In that context, it does not matter whether the claimant is disadvantaged along with others or not, and it cannot in any way weaken her case with respect to justification that her beliefs are not more widely shared or do not constitute a core belief of any particular religion [35].

He went on to state that the Article 9 dimension

> made it inappropriate for the Employment Tribunal, when assessing justification, to weigh in the employer's favour the fact that the appellant's religious belief was not a core belief of her religion so that any group impact was limited [37].

Talking about Religion at Work

In *Drew*,[126] the claimant was a paediatric consultant in a multicultural, multi-faith hospital department who habitually used Christian references in pro-

126 *Drew v Walsall Healthcare NHS Trust* [2013] UKEAT 0378/12/2009.

fessional communications. An internal investigation recommended that he should keep his personal and religious views to himself [16]; and when he refused to do so, he was dismissed [32]. The EAT held that he had not been treated less favourably because of his Christian beliefs. The Employment Tribunal had correctly applied the guidance set out by the EAT in *Ladele*[127] and had identified the correct hypothetical comparator: someone whose relevant circumstances were the same as the claimant's (save for his protected characteristic as an 'orthodox Christian') and who had acted in the same way as the claimant but in terms relating to that person's own belief system—whether religious or non-religious [58 & 59].

In *Wasteney*,[128] a senior occupational therapist had been given a final written warning (subsequently reduced on appeal to a first written warning) for three charges of misconduct: praying with EN, a more junior Muslim colleague of Pakistani heritage, giving her a book about a Muslim woman who converts to Christianity and inviting her to church events. The Employment Tribunal held that there had been no element of harassment or discrimination in the Trust's response to EN's complaint; though Article 9 ECHR was engaged, the Convention did not give Ms Wasteney 'a complete and unfettered right to discuss or act on her religious beliefs at work irrespective of the views of others or her employer …' [67].

The decision was upheld on appeal.[129] HHJ Eady, sitting alone, concluded that Ms Wasteney

> had not been subjected to disciplinary process or sanction because she manifested her religious belief in voluntary and consensual exchanges with a colleague but because … she subjected a subordinate to unwanted and unwelcome conduct, going substantially beyond 'religious discussion', without regard to her own influential position. The treatment of which the claimant complained was because of, and related to, those inappropriate actions; not any legitimate manifestation of her belief [65].

Similarly in *Kuteh*,[130] patients complained that a nursing sister who was a 'committed Christian' talked about religion when she was assessing them [22]. After a discussion with the Matron—which was confirmed in writing—she

---

127 *Islington v Ladele* [2008] UKEAT 0453/08/1912.

128 *Wasteney v East London NHS Foundation Trust* [2015] ET 3200658/2014.

129 *Wasteney v East London NHS Foundation Trust* [2016] UKEAT 0157/15/0704.

130 *Mrs S Kuteh v Dartford and Gravesham NHS Trust (England and Wales: Unfair Dismissal)* [2017] UKET 2302764/2016.

undertook to change her ways [23]. However, she relapsed, there were further complaints and she was ultimately suspended for repeated misconduct, inappropriate behaviour and breach of the nursing and midwifery code [25 & 26]. Finally, after a formal investigation meeting, she was dismissed [26–37]. The Employment Tribunal concluded that the internal appeal process had been thorough, fair and reasonable and that the subsequent confirmation of her dismissal was unimpeachable [81]. Because she had not made a claim under Article 9 ECHR, it was not in play [82]; but she had been prevented from *inappropriately proselytising* her beliefs, as opposed to being prevented from manifesting them—hence her dismissal [83 & 84]. Nor had the Trust breached her Article 9 rights [85]. Her claim was dismissed.

Finally, in *Trayhorn*,[131] a gardener/horticulturalist at HM Prison Littlehey, who happened also to be an ordained Pentecostal minister, spoke to a congregation of prisoners at a Pentecostal service in the prison chapel in May 2014 about homosexuality as a sin, quoting from 1 Corinthians 6: 9–11. He had done so on a previous occasion, one of the prisoners present at that service had made a formal complaint and Mr Trayhorn had been told that he was not to preach in the chapel in future. Finally, he was dismissed and claimed indirect religious discrimination.

Before the EAT, it was argued that that the Employment Tribunal had been wrong to hold that his dismissal had not been 'because of' or 'related to' his religion or belief' because, under *Eweida*,[132] the test was whether there was a 'sufficiently close and direct nexus between the act and the underlying belief'. The ET had also erred in relying on group disadvantage as a necessary condition for Mr Trayhorn to establish indirect discrimination because, it was argued, where Article 9 ECHR was engaged, proof of group disadvantage was not required [45]. Finally, it was suggested that the ET had failed to undertake 'a proper balancing act' between Mr Trayhorn's rights under Articles 9 and 10 ECHR and the proposed limitation of those rights, particularly in the light of the principle of church independence [82].

Slade J dismissed the appeal. She did not accept counsel's interpretation of the connection between the disputed act of the Prison Service and Mr Trayhorn's protected characteristic [42]. Moreover, the ET had found as a fact—against which there could be no appeal—that no part of the Prison Service's Conduct and Disciplinary Policy or Equality of Treatment of Employees Policy had been identified as putting either Mr Trayhorn as an individual,

---

131 *Trayhorn v The Secretary of State for Justice (Religion or Belief Discrimination)* [2017] UKEAT 0304/16/0108.

132 *Eweida & Ors v United Kingdom* [2013] ECHR 37 [82].

Pentecostals in particular or Christians in general at a disadvantage, whether singly or as a group [79]. Finally, the ET had given proper weight to the restraint on Mr Trayhorn's expression of his religious beliefs when it decided that, in the circumstances, the Prison Service's application of its Discipline and Equalities Policies had been a proportionate means of achieving a legitimate aim [93].

Time Off for Religious Observance

In *Cherfi*,[133] a Muslim security guard had been refused permission to leave the site to which he was assigned to attend midday Friday prayers at a nearby mosque. Though G4S was concerned that, apart from financial penalties, the contract would be in danger if a full complement of security staff was not on site at all times, it had offered him a variety of alternatives, such as Saturday or Sunday working, which he had refused. There was also a prayer room available to him on site—though that did not meet his desire to attend prayers as part of a congregation. The lower tribunal had held that he was not prevented from working on Fridays and, though he was offered weekend work at other sites so that he would not suffer financially if he chose not to work on Fridays, he had not been pressurised to work on Saturdays and Sundays. The EAT upheld the balancing exercise carried out by the lower tribunal and dismissed his appeal.

Most recently in *Gareddu*,[134] a Roman Catholic from Sardinia claimed that his religious beliefs required him to go back to Sardinia every year for approximately five weeks around August to take part in religious festivals with his family [3]. Until 2013, London Underground allowed him to do so but in 2013 he was told 'not again'. He lost in a grievance procedure and an internal appeal, In the EAT he appealed the ET's conclusion that he had not suffered unlawful indirect discrimination on the grounds that the ET had not applied the proper approach to his claim of indirect discrimination under s 19 Equality Act 2010 (read together with Article 9 ECHR), had imposed an unwarranted additional requirement that 'religion' should be his sole or primary motivation in order to attract the protection of s 19, had considered an irrelevant factor—his desire to worship collectively with his family—in determining whether he had acted in good faith and had been perverse in its construction of his evidence-in-chief.

Simler J dismissed the appeal. Perhaps the most telling point of her judgment was that his demands were disproportionate:

---

133 *Cherfi v G4S Security Services Ltd* [2011] UKEAT 0379/10/2405.

134 *Gareddu v London Underground Ltd* [2016] UKEAT 0086/16/1512.

> The mere fact that attendance at a single festival is a genuine manifestation of religious belief does not inevitably mean that attendance for a five-week period to do so is also a genuine manifestation [31].

So Where Does One Draw the Line?

It might be assumed from the foregoing that the scope for religious manifestation in the workplace is extremely restricted—but the traffic is not entirely one way. In *Holland*,[135] a follower of Wicca worked at a convenience store operated by a company owned by the second respondent, Mr Tarloch Singh, a Sikh. In October 2012 Ms Holland agreed with her manager that she would work a late shift so that she could celebrate Halloween. Next day, Mr Singh asked her why she was working a later shift and she described his reaction to her explanation as 'seeming revolted by the idea that she was a Wiccan, or not Christian, and [she] was made to feel that there was something wrong with her' [10.2]. In due course she was dismissed, ostensibly on the grounds that the company was reducing its workforce and her post was being eliminated, even though a male colleague was retained [10.7]. There was the usual dispute as to the facts; but the Employment Tribunal preferred Ms Holland's version and upheld her claim.

In *Mbuyi*[136] the claimant, an Evangelical Christian, was employed at a nursery in Shepherds Bush: her colleague Laura P was a lesbian in a civil partnership. There were various complaints, most particularly in relation to comments that Ms Mbuyi was alleged to have made to Ms P about her sexual orientation, such as 'Oh my God, are you a lesbian?'. She was dismissed and brought a claim under the Equality Act 2010, alleging that her dismissal was an act of direct or unjustified indirect discrimination and/or harassment, relying on the protected characteristic of her religion or belief and, specifically, on her religious belief that homosexuality was a sin [97 & 98].

The Employment Tribunal found in Ms Mbuyi's favour. The Tribunal rejected the charge that her belief was 'discriminatory, homophobic and akin to racism' [124]. There was a difference between, for example, a racist expressing hateful views and a person of religious conviction expressing her beliefs, 'however unwelcome', though that was not to suggest that 'the inappropriate expression of religious beliefs that may appear discriminatory would receive special protection under the law' [125].

---

135 *Holland v Angel Supermarket Ltd & Anor* [2013] ET 3301005/2013.

136 *Mbuyi v Newpark Childcare (Shepherds Bush) Ltd* [2015] ET 3300656/2014.

Similarly in *Fhima*,[137] the claimant, an observant Jew, applied for a vacancy with a car rental firm, Travel Jigsaw, which required the successful applicant to work shifts on five out of every seven days. When Travel Jigsaw refused to employ Ms Fhima, she explained that she could not work during *Shabbat* but, because the company ran a 24/7 operation, she offered to work every Sunday and from 5pm to midnight on Saturdays in winter and asked Jigsaw to review its refusal. The Tribunal held that the requirement that Ms Fhima be available to work on Saturdays was not an objective justification for a policy that discriminated against observant Jews. Other staff could have covered the Saturday shifts with Ms Fhima working on five of the other six days.

Most recently, in *Kiss*,[138] the claimant, a refrigeration engineer and a practising Roman Catholic, had an altercation with his employer over what he alleged had been incorrect installation of a freezer for a client [79]. He was summoned to a meeting—which he covertly recorded—with the third respondent, Mr Rajive Sachdev, who shouted and swore at him, banged his fist on the table and told him that, though he 'called himself a good Christian man ... it was bullshit because the Claimant would not know the word good if it came and smacked him in the face' and that that according to Mr Kiss everybody else was in the wrong—the manufacturer, the engineers and even God—and he, Kiss, was always right. He added 'You are almighty Jesus Christ' and referred to him as 'Mr Jesus Christ, educated best engineer in the world' [32]. Before the Employment Tribunal, Mr Kiss alleged direct discrimination and harassment on grounds of religion.

The Tribunal found that the comments about Mr Kiss not recognising good if it smacked him in the face and believing that he was always right and everyone else, including God, was wrong were 'not insulting or offensive about or denigrating of Christianity or, indeed, religion at all' [48]: essentially, they were a personal criticism of Mr Kiss. However, the references to Jesus Christ were different: Mr Sachdev had used a religious figure who was important to Mr Kiss because of his religion to demean and insult him. It had been inappropriate behaviour and it had been reasonable for him, as a devout, practising Roman Catholic, to be offended by Mr Sachdev's behaviour [49]. It concluded that, though not every offensive remark amounted to harassment, on balance those two remarks had just crossed the threshold of religious harassment [49]. Given that it was a one-off incident and that Mr Sachdev had apologised at the

137 *Fhima v Travel Jigsaw Ltd* [2015] ET (unreported).

138 *Mr R Kiss v Dephna Estates Ltd and others* [2017] UKET 2205945/2016.

hearing, the case fell into the lowest band of the *Vento*[139] guidelines and the Tribunal awarded £3,000.

The Need for Caution

If there is a lesson to be learned it is this: if employees need to be exceedingly careful about the religious sensibilities of their colleagues, equally, employers (and that includes religious employers) need to equally cautious about the religious sensitivities of their employees. That said, however, I would suggest that it would be wise for employees not to rely too strongly on the conclusion in *Mbuyi*.

Vicarious Liability and Historic Sexual Abuse

Historic Sexual Abuse Claims

The growth in historic physical and sexual abuse claims, some of them relating to matters alleged to have taken place decades ago, has raised questions about the extent to which religious institutions are vicariously liable for alleged abuses committed by people under their control, whether employees, office holders or volunteers.

Maga and *JGE*

In *Maga*,[140] the Court of Appeal held the Archdiocese of Birmingham vicariously liable for the activities of one of its priests whom it had not supervised adequately and who had sexually abused a boy. Mr Maga was not a Roman Catholic and had not worshipped at the church, but when he was a boy he had washed the priest's car and had attended parish social events. The Court held the Archdiocese vicariously liable even though it had reserved its position as to whether or not the offending priest was an 'employee' and Mr Maga was not and had not been an adherent of the Church.[141]

Next, in *JGE*,[142] the claimant alleged that when she was resident at a children's home in Hampshire between 1970 and 1972 she had been raped by one

139 *Vento v Chief Constable of West Yorkshire Police* [2002] EWCA Civ 1871, in which the Court of Appeal set out guidelines for how much compensation should be awarded in respect of injury to feeling.

140 *Maga v Trustees of the Birmingham Archdiocese of the Roman Catholic Church* [2010] EWCA Civ 256.

141 For two slightly different views on *Maga*, see Cranmer (2011) and Hall (2011).

142 *JGE v English Province of Our Lady of Charity & Anor* [2011] EWHC 2871 (QB).

Father Baldwin, a Roman Catholic priest who had since died. The issue before the court was whether the second defendant—the Trustees of the Portsmouth Roman Catholic Diocesan Trust—might be vicariously liable for Baldwin's alleged torts. Following the reasoning in *Maga* and in a Canadian case on very similar facts, *Doe*,[143] the High Court found for the claimant:

> By appointing [*sic*] Father Baldwin as a priest, and thus clothing him with all the powers involved, the defendants created a risk of harm to others, viz the risk that he could abuse or misuse those powers for his own purposes or otherwise'. [39]

The Trustees of the Diocese appealed; and the Court of Appeal upheld the original decision by two to one.[144] Permission to appeal to the Supreme Court was refused—but the refusal was on the grounds that the SC was shortly to hear yet another vicarious liability appeal from the Court of Appeal's decision in *Various Claimants*.[145]

Various Claimants

The Supreme Court duly heard the appeal in *Various Claimants*,[146] in which it addressed the issue of vicarious liability for historic sexual abuse. The crux of the appeal was whether or not the Institute, a lay religious order founded to educate children, was vicariously liable for alleged acts of sexual and physical abuse by its members between 1952 and 1992 at St William's School—a residential institution in Market Weighton for boys in need of care. The Institute did not own the school. In 1973, it became an assisted community home for children in the care of the local authority, managed by the Middlesbrough Diocesan Rescue Society until 1982 and thereafter by the Catholic Child Welfare Society (Diocese of Middlesbrough). In 1990 the headmaster, Brother James, was expelled from the Institute after it was discovered he was guilty of systematic sexual abuse of boys in his care and in 1993 and 2004 he was convicted of numerous sexual offences against boys over a period of 20 years. The School was closed in 1994.

143 *Doe v Bennett & Ors* 2004 SCC 17.

144 *JGE v Portsmouth Roman Catholic Diocesan Trust* [2012] EWCA Civ 938.

145 *Various Claimants v The Catholic Child Welfare Society and the Institute of Brothers of the Christian Schools & Ors* [2010] EWCA Civ 1106.

146 *Catholic Child Welfare Society & Ors v Various Claimants and The Institute of the Brothers of the Christian Schools* [2012] UKSC 56.

170 men brought claims for damages in respect of alleged abuse from 1973 onwards against the managers of the school (the 'Middlesbrough Defendants', who had inherited the statutory liabilities of the former managers and had entered into contracts of employment with the teachers, who were Christian Brothers) and against the Institute itself. The brothers who taught at the school were not bound in contract to the Institute but to the Middlesbrough Defendants. As a preliminary issue, the High Court held—and the Court of Appeal confirmed—that the Institute was not vicariously liable for the tortious acts committed by Christian Brothers at the school. The Middlesbrough Defendants appealed to the Supreme Court on a preliminary point, arguing that vicarious liability should be shared between them and the Institute.

The Supreme Court allowed the appeal. Delivering the judgment of the Court, Lord Phillips of Worth Matravers PSC explained that

> the law ... rendered the employer, D2, liable for the tortious act of the employee, D1, provided that the act in question was committed 'in the course of the employee's employment' Thus, in a case about vicarious liability, the focus was on two stages: (1) was there a true relationship of employer/employee between D2 and D1? (2) was D1 acting in the course of his employment when he committed the tortious act? [19]

He enunciated the test for vicarious liability as:

> a synthesis of two stages: (i) The first stage is to consider the relationship of D1 and D2 to see whether it is one that is capable of giving rise to vicarious liability. (ii) ... What is critical at the second stage is the connection that links the relationship between D1 and D2 and the act or omission of D1 [21].

He concluded:

- that the necessary relationship between the brothers and the Institute and the close connection between that relationship and the abuse committed at the school had been made out [88];
- that the relationship between the brothers and the Institute was much closer to that of employment than the relationship between the priest and the bishop in *JGE* [89];
- that the business and mission of the Institute—Christian education for boys—was the common business and mission of every brother who was a member of it [89 & 90];

- that the relationship between the Institute and the brothers enabled the Institute to place the brothers in teaching positions and, in particular, in the position of headmaster at St William's and there was a very close connection between the relationship between the brothers and the Institute and the employment of the brothers as teachers in the school [91];
- that the children at the school were vulnerable [92]; and
- that there was a very close connection between the brothers' employment as teachers and the alleged sexual abuse [93].

In short:

> This is not a borderline case. It is one where it is fair, just and reasonable, by reason of the satisfaction of the relevant criteria, for the Institute to share with the Middlesbrough Defendants vicarious liability for the abuse committed by the brothers [84].[147]

Time-Barred Caims

In some circumstances, vicarious liability can apply to incidents that occurred so long ago that they have almost been forgotten by the employer—which is one of the principal criticisms of those who feel that the law on vicarious liability has drifted too far in the direction of claimants.

In *Raggett*,[148] the Governors of a school accepted vicarious liability for the activities of a Jesuit schoolteacher alleged to have sexually abused a pupil; however, they argued that the case was time-barred under the Limitation Act 1980. The Court of Appeal held that, nevertheless, even though the complaint was time-barred, the judge at first instance had properly exercised her discretion under s.33 of the Limitation Act 1980 in allowing the action to proceed. Similarly, in *Watchtower Bible and Tract Society*,[149] the Court was prepared to hold the Jehovah's Witnesses liable for sexual assaults on Ms A, now 29, carried out by one Peter Stewart from 1989 to 1994 when she was between about 4

147 At the time of writing, the hearing of the substantive issues was taking place before the High Court.

148 *Raggett v Society of Jesus Trust of 1929 for Roman Catholic Purposes & Anor* [2010] EWCA Civ 1002. For a recent Irish case on joint and several vicarious liability, see *Hickey v McGowan & Ors* [2017] IESC 6, in which the Supreme Court, Charleton J dissenting, overturned the High Court and held that the Marist Order, though an unincorporated body, was vicariously liable *separately from its members* for sexual abuse perpetrated by Cosgrove, the second defendant, who at the time of the abuse was a Marist Brother. There is a helpful summary on the Supreme Court of Ireland blog (Anon, 2017).

149 *A v Watchtower Bible and Tract Society (Trustees of) & Ors* [2015] EWHC 1722 (QB).

and 9. It did so despite the fact that the action was out of time under the Limitation Act 1980 and Stewart, a 'ministerial assistant', did not have any employment relationship with the Witnesses.

Watchtower Bible and Tract Society is completely in line with recent cases, all of which suggest that judges have become very reluctant to conclude that a survivor of sexual abuse should not be compensated, even if the perpetrator is dead or was not an employee of the organisation that is being sued. It may possibly be the case, however, that the courts are becoming more reluctant to allow extensions of time in relation to very old allegations.

In the recent case of *F and S*,[150] the two claimants sought damages as victims of sexual abuse, which, they alleged, was perpetrated by Father M between 1979 and 1986. The defendants were sued as personal representatives of the Bishop then responsible for the diocese in which Father M worked as a priest. It was accepted (in effect on behalf of the local Roman Catholic Church) that the Bishop was vicariously liable for such acts of abuse as might be established; but the defendants argued successfully that, because at least 30 years had passed since the last alleged acts of abuse, they could not now be proved to the requisite standard of proof—the civil standard of the balance of probabilities—and that the passage of time had rendered the testimony unreliable and made it difficult to assess fairly [2]. The primary limitation period under the Limitation Act 1980 had expired; and Langstaff J refused the application for an extension because:

> although it is entirely possible that one or both of the claimants may have been the subject of serious abuse and breach of trust by a priest for whose deeds the defendant is vicariously liable I do not think that a fair trial of these allegations is any longer possible [87].

That said, however, it cannot be emphasised too strongly that, again, any case involving vicarious liability for sexual abuse is highly sensitive to its facts. Just because Langstaff J refused an extension in *F and S* does not mean that another judge would not allow an extension in another case.

'The Law of Vicarious Liability is on the Move'

Finally on this point, where an organist or caretaker/verger (say) who undertakes duties for a congregation through its PCC, congregational board or

150 *F and S v TH* [2016] EWHC 1605 (QB).

trustees commits a tort or delict,[151] that congregation may find itself held vicariously liable even if the miscreant has only limited rights for the purposes of employment protection legislation.

The Supreme Court has handed down two linked judgments on vicarious liability which it described as complementary to each other: *Cox*[152] and *Mohamud*.[153] *Cox* addresses the degree of connection between the defendant organisation, the wrongdoer and the impugned act that is necessary for vicarious liability to arise, while *Mohamud* is about the degree of connection between the defendant and the wrongdoer that is required to make the defendant vicariously liable for the wrongdoer's actions.

In *Cox*, the tortfeasor was a prisoner and could not possibly have been held to be 'employed' by the Prison Service in the sense understood by employment protection legislation, even though he was working in the prison kitchen and paid a nominal wage. Lord Reed made it clear, however, that

> It is sufficient [to establish liability] that there is a defendant which is carrying on activities in the furtherance of its own interests. The individual for whose conduct it may be vicariously liable must carry on activities assigned to him by the defendant as an integral part of its operation and for its benefit. The defendant must, by assigning those activities to him, have created a risk of his committing the tort ... a wide range of circumstances can satisfy those requirements ... *defendants cannot avoid vicarious liability on the basis of technical arguments about the employment status of the individual who committed the tort* [31 & 32: emphasis added].

Cox and *Mohamud*, taken together, limit even further the degree to which a defendant organisation can argue successfully that a miscreant employee *or agent* was acting outside its control and they underline the fact that whether or not an organisation is vicariously liable for a tort is not dependent on the

151 The Kilbrandon Report on children and young persons in Scotland (1964, republished 2003) says this at Appendix B about vicarious liability in Scots law: '[A] defender may be vicariously liable for the act of another although he himself has not been in fault at all. Thus the employer of a servant who commits a delict in the course of his employment is liable in damages, although he is not personally involved in the delict and has taken all proper care to choose a competent servant. Vicarious liability, defined in this way, is a comparatively modem development, and was adopted in Scots law only in the nineteenth century'.

152 *Cox v Ministry of Justice* [2016] UKSC 10.

153 *Mohamud v WM Morrison Supermarkets plc* [2016] UKSC 11.

tortfeasor having employment rights. Or as Lord Reed put it in *Cox*, 'The law of vicarious liability is on the move ... It has not yet come to a stop' [1].

Reasonable Accommodation?

Discrimination and 'Protected Characteristics'

As noted earlier, under the terms of the Equality Act 2010 and the previous legislation that it subsumed, there are two kinds of discrimination: direct and indirect. *Direct* discrimination occurs where an employer treats someone who has a 'protected characteristic'—age, disability, gender reassignment, sexual orientation, marriage and civil partnership, pregnancy and maternity, race, religion or belief and sex—less favourably that others are treated (or would be treated) because of that characteristic. *Indirect* discrimination occurs when an organisation's practices, policies or procedures have the effect of disadvantaging people who share certain protected characteristics: where the employer applies a 'provision, criterion or practice' (PCP) to someone which discriminates against that person's protected characteristic.

So in the case of religion, a PCP in employment is discriminatory where:

- it applies to persons with whom the claimant does not share a religion or belief;
- it puts, or would put, persons with whom the claimant shares a religion or belief at a particular disadvantage when compared with others;
- it puts, or would put, the claimant at that disadvantage; and
- the employer cannot demonstrate that it is a proportionate means of achieving a legitimate aim.

There is no objective justification that can be pleaded in circumstances of direct discrimination, except possibly where age is a relevant factor. *Indirect* discrimination, on the other hand, may not be unlawful if an employer can show that there was an objective justification for the PCP that it applied to its employees. But in order to demonstrate that the PCP complained of was justifiable and proportionate, the employer must demonstrate that there was no reasonable, less discriminatory alternative to the course of action pursued.

So in *Mba*, for example, Maurice Kay LJ found there had been an error of law in the decisions of the lower tribunals [20] but nevertheless concluded that requiring Mrs Mba to work on certain Sundays was a proportionate means of achieving an indisputably legitimate aim: the effective operation of Brightwell children's home 24 hours a day, seven days a week [24].

Ms Mba, however, had claimed that her employer could have accommodated her religious convictions about not working on Sundays without affecting the running of the children's home: in short, she was arguing for some sort of 'reasonable accommodation'.

Whether or not some form of reasonable accommodation is desirable—or even possible—is by no means uncontroversial. In *Bull*,[154] which was about the refusal by two avowedly-Christian hotelkeepers to let a double room to a couple in a civil partnership, Lady Hale DPSC was

> more than ready to accept that the scope for reasonable accommodation is part of the proportionality assessment, at least in some cases. This is reinforced by the decision in *Eweida v United Kingdom* (2013) 57 EHRR 8, where the Strasbourg court abandoned its previous stance that there was no interference with an employee's right to manifest her religion if it could be avoided by changing jobs. Rather, that possibility was to be taken into account in the overall proportionality assessment, which must therefore consider the extent to which it is reasonable to expect the employer to accommodate the employee's right [47].

But she nevertheless concluded that Mr and Mrs Bull could not 'get round the fact that United Kingdom law prohibits them from doing as they did' [51].

Matthew Gibson (2013: 589) has argued that while religious believers 'cannot expect *carte blanche* dispensation' from their employers' requirements, recent judgments 'pose on-going concerns about the level of protection such individuals receive in UK anti-discrimination law'. Erica Howard (2013: 365–370), on the other hand, regards the tests of group disadvantage and justification under indirect discrimination as providing sufficient protection.

The matter is complicated by the fact that there is no definitive guidance as to what constitutes a 'group' for the purpose of demonstrating group disadvantage. In *Chatwal*,[155] for example, a baptised Sikh claimed that he could not take part in the rota to clean the refrigerator in the communal staff kitchen because his religion forbade him to touch meat. Mr Recorder Luba QC observed that the task of determining whether or not the claimant had discharged the burden of showing that there was a group of Sikhs who shared his religious belief about touching meat

154 *Bull & Anor v Hall & Anor* [2013] UKSC 73.

155 *Chatwal v Wandsworth Borough Council (Religion or Belief Discrimination)* [2011] UKEAT 0487/10/0607.

> was not helped by the fact that there is no consensus in law as to how large (or small) this cohort of others or 'group' must be in order to suffice [25].

Reasonable accommodation was given considerable impetus, however, when Lady Hale returned to it in two lectures in 2014 at Yale Law School (2014a) and at the Law Society of Ireland (2014b). In the second, she asked:

> [S]hould we be developing, in both human rights and EU law, an explicit requirement upon the providers of employment, goods and services to make reasonable accommodation for the manifestation of religious and other beliefs? And even *vice versa*? (2014b: 16).

She concluded:

> [I]f the law is going to protect freedom of religion and belief it has to accept that all religions and beliefs and none are equal. It cannot realistically inquire into the validity or importance of those beliefs, or any particular manifestation of them, as long as they are genuinely held. It then has to work out how far it should go in making special provisions or exceptions for particular beliefs, how far it should require the providers of employments, goods and services to accommodate them, and how far it should allow for a 'conscience clause', either to the providers ... or to employees ... I am not sure that our law has yet found a reasonable accommodation of all these different strands. The story has just begun (2014b: 20).

Her call was echoed in January 2015 by Resolution 2036 of the Parliamentary Assembly of the Council of Europe, on *Tackling intolerance and discrimination in Europe with a special focus on Christians*, based on a Report by the Assembly's Committee on Equality and Non-Discrimination. The Resolution called on states parties, *inter alia*, to promote a culture of tolerance and 'living together' based on the acceptance of religious pluralism, the contribution of religions to a democratic and pluralist society and the right of individuals not to adhere to any religion, to promote reasonable accommodation within the principle of indirect discrimination so as to ensure respect for the right of all individuals under their jurisdiction to freedom of religion and belief 'without impairing for anyone the other rights also guaranteed by the European Convention on Human Rights' and to uphold freedom of conscience in the workplace 'while ensuring that access to services provided by law is maintained and the right of others to be free from discrimination is protected'.[156]

Most recently, the call has been taken up by Katayoun Alidadi, who argues that the introduction of reasonable accommodation would give important additional protection and guarantees to employees who face work conditions that compete with their religious commitments. She suggests that it would provide tangible benefits by 'correcting legal-technical limitations and shortcomings' in the application of human rights and non-discrimination law, because it would dispense with the requirement to demonstrate group disadvantage and the comparison of the claimant with other employees: the problem highlighted by Mr Recorder Luba in *Chatwal*. It would also have the *intangible* benefit of giving employers, employees and society at large 'an alternative language to address tension between legitimate needs' (2017: 265). In short, the question would be, 'Is this a reasonable request that will not impose a disproportionate burden on the employer?'

One can see considerable merit in exploring this further: however, one can also see considerable problems, the most obvious of which is the competing interests of the various actors in a particular workplace: the claimant, the employer, the claimant's colleagues and the customers or service-users may all have different rights that clamour for recognition.

How, for example, could Kirklees Council have 'reasonably accommodated' Ms Azmi's wish to wear a *niqab* veil at work when her school was convinced that it would hinder communication with the children in her charge? Either she could wear it or she could not: the possible middle course of allowing her to wear it *except* when she was in the classroom was probably unrealistic. Similarly, to what extent can an employer object to a particular hairstyle worn on religious or cultural grounds? In *Harris*,[157] the EAT concluded that the claimant, a Rastafarian, had been dismissed not because he wore dreadlocks but because the company's dress-code required that their drivers 'should have a smart professional haircut and should ensure hair is tidy' [12]—and Mr Harris's hair was not.[158]

---

156 It should be noted in passing that the concept of 'living together' (which is *not* in the Convention) seems to have sneaked its way into the Resolution—possibly from the judgment in *S.A.S. v France* noted earlier. It should also be remembered that Resolutions of the Parliamentary Assembly are not binding on the Council of Ministers.

157 *Harris v NKL Automotive Ltd & Anor* [2007] UKEAT 0134/07/0310.

158 In *G v St Gregory's Catholic Science College* [2011] EWHC 1452 (Admin) on the other hand, the Administrative Court held that the school's prohibition on boys (but not girls) wearing

Or what if the claimant rejects any offer of compromise? 'Reasonable accommodation' assumes that both parties are prepared to be 'reasonable'; in matters of religion, however, individuals sometimes elevate particular issues to matters of principle on which compromise is simply not possible. In *Chaplin*, for example, when Mrs Chaplin's manager requested her to remove her neck-chain and crucifix she refused, insisting that the crucifix was a religious symbol. When her supervisors suggested that she might secure her crucifix and chain to the lanyard holding her identity badge, she refused their offer because she would still be required to remove her badge and lanyard when performing close clinical duties.[159] What more could her employer have done at that point other than to admit defeat?

In an earlier case, *Cherfi*,[160] a Muslim security guard had been refused permission to leave the site to which he was assigned to attend midday Friday prayers at a nearby mosque. Though G4S was concerned that, apart from financial penalties, the contract would be in danger if a full complement of security staff was not on site at all times, it had offered him a variety of alternatives, such as Saturday or Sunday working, which he had refused. There was also a prayer room available to him on site—though that did not meet his desire to attend prayers as part of a congregation. The lower tribunal had held that he was not prevented from working on Fridays and, though he was offered weekend work at other sites so that he would not suffer financially if he chose not to work on Fridays, he had not been pressurised to work on Saturdays and Sundays. The EAT upheld the balancing exercise carried out by the lower tribunal and dismissed his appeal.

That is not to say that reasonable accommodation is never possible. As we have already seen, for example, the Employment Tribunal held in *Fhima* that Travel Jigsaw could not provide an objective justification for a policy that would require Ms Fhima be available to work on Saturdays and which discriminated against observant Jews. In doing so, it was no doubt influenced by the fact that Ms Fhima had offered her own 'reasonable accommodation': to work every Sunday and to work from 5pm to midnight on Saturdays in winter, when *Shabbat* had ended.

---

their hair in cornrows constituted unjustifiable indirect discrimination against an Afro-Caribbean boy refused a place at the school—but *G* was not an employment case because the boy was a prospective pupil, not an employee.

159 *Eweida and Others v United Kingdom* [2013] ECHR 37 [20].

160 *Cherfi v G4S Security Services Ltd* [2011] UKEAT 0379/10/2405.

The Canadian Model

Canada has a specific test of reasonable accommodation that was enunciated in *O'Malley*;[161] and Matthew Gibson (2013: 595) offers it as a possible way forward for the UK. The claimant, Mrs O'Malley, was first employed by Simpsons-Sears in 1971 and had become a Seventh-Day Adventist in 1978; henceforward, she had been obliged to keep the Sabbath from sunset on Friday to sunset on Saturday and could no longer work on Saturdays. It was common ground that her conversion was genuine, sincere and in no way actuated by any desire to procure more favourable working conditions. It was also common ground that the policy of Saturday opening was for sound business reasons and was not intended to discriminate against Mrs O'Malley or her coreligionists. In allowing her appeal, the Supreme Court set out the following two-stage test:

- The complainant must show a *prima facie* case of discrimination which covers the allegations made 'and which, if they are believed, is complete and sufficient to justify a verdict in the complainant's favour in the absence of an answer from the respondent employer' [25].
- 'Where adverse effect discrimination on the basis of creed is shown and the offending rule is rationally connected to the performance of the job', the onus of proof is on the employer to demonstrate that 'he has taken such reasonable steps toward accommodation of the employee's position as are open to him without undue hardship' [28].[162]

Applying that test, Mrs Chaplin, Mr Cherfi and Mr McFarlane would probably still have been unsuccessful. Gibson suggests, however (2013: 604ff), that the Canadian model could have provided a pragmatic solution to accommodate the unfortunate Ms Ladele. Mark Hill (2013) agrees:

> An unanticipated and unilateral change in a fundamental term of her employment gave her a stark choice: to act against her religious convictions (which the court accepted were conscientiously and sincerely held) or to leave her employment. With creative rostering, Ladele's convictions could have been accommodated by Islington without any detriment to the registration of civil partnerships in the Borough.

161 *Ontario Human Rights Commission (O'Malley) v Simpsons-Sears* 1985 CanLII 18 (SCC).

162 *O'Malley* [28], *per* McIntyre J.

Ultimately, whether or not a proposed accommodation was 'reasonable' would fall to be determined on the facts. In *Copsey*, for example, Neuberger LJ in the Court of Appeal endorsed the view of the Employment Tribunal that

> Devon Clays had done everything they reasonably could have done or could have been expected to do, in the particular circumstances of the case, to accommodate Mr Copsey's desire not to work on Sundays ... if the Employment Tribunal thought anyone had acted unreasonably in this case, it was Mr Copsey [96].

A Simpler Alternative?

Recently, the Equality and Human Rights Commission has published updated guidance on religion and belief in the workplace and an accompanying legal analysis, *Religion or belief—is the law working?* Its concludes that the existing model of indirect discrimination and the concept of balancing rights provide sufficient protection for manifesting religion or belief and that the current legislation should not be amended to impose a new duty of reasonable accommodation (EHRC: 2016, 40).

Lucy Vickers has proposed a simpler alternative: something analogous to the current right to request flexible working (2016: 272). She suggests that this would be the better model: a request that the employer would be obliged to consider but not bound to grant. She is doubtful that a separate and explicit duty of reasonable accommodation would materially change the level of protection available for religion or belief in the workplace, but feels that a duty on the lines of the flexible working provisions would clarify individual rights by abolishing the requirement to find comparators. Instead, each application would have to be assessed on its own merits, without any need to demonstrate generalised group disadvantage. She also believes that a right to request would be 'more intuitive and straightforward for employees' and might also prove more acceptable to workers because the process would be less confrontational than having to bring a claim for indirect discrimination. How much of a burden it would prove to be for employers would depend on how high the bar was set for refusal by the employer on grounds of hardship: in the United States, it happens to be set very low.

But, as Lady Hale said in her lecture to the Law Society of Ireland, 'The story has just begun'.

So Just How Far Can You Go?

To conclude: a cautionary tale from Canada that did not reach the courts. A Muslim man joined an aikido class. First, he refused to bow to other students in accordance with the custom in Japanese martial arts because his religion prohibited it. Next, he told the teacher that it was against his religion to touch females, so the class would have to be segregated to accommodate him: *and so it was*. A lawyer for the Nova Scotia Human Rights Commission refused to comment on the aikido case specifically but acknowledged the general problem of competing rights: 'In the fabric of Canadian society, [gender segregation] isn't something that, in a secular sense, we support ... we generally see it as a bad thing' (Hopper, 2014). But she pointed out that the law also required reasonable accommodation of religious views and that they were generally given much higher consideration than matters of mere personal preference.

So what we have here is a clash between gender equality as guaranteed by s.15(1) of the Charter of Rights and Freedoms in Part I of Canada's Constitution Act 1982 and the Muslim man's perceived right to practise aikido without coming into contact with females. Said the Commission's lawyer: 'If it doesn't cost us to the point of undue hardship, then we need to try to ... support [people of faith] and not have them feel persecuted for their deeply-held belief'.

Which is fair enough, so far as it goes: but at what point does accommodation become 'undue hardship'? And at what point does religious principle shade into sheer bloody-mindedness? Is there a *human right* to practise aikido without coming into contact with a member of the opposite sex? And if the man in question wanted to practise a body-contact sport and to do so in accordance with his religious principles, why not a sport like boxing or wrestling that is strictly segregated as a matter of course? Or, since he was in Canada, ice-hockey?

In Conclusion

Employment Law in a State of Flux

If there is any conclusion at all to be drawn from all that has gone before, perhaps it is this: that the law on religion in relation to matters such as employment, vicarious liability and the right to manifest beliefs in the workplace is in a constant state of flux. As suggested at the outset, employment law has become extremely complicated. The 'servant of God' approach seems to have withered away; but perhaps the next issue will be whether the distinctions between employees, workers and office holders and between contracts of employment, contracts of service and contracts for services are either helpful or likely to lead to a rational conclusion in every individual case.

On clergy employment in particular, it may be that the Supreme Court judgment in *Preston* has halted the tendency to find an employment relationship where none was intended by the Church in question and has moderated the influence of *Percy*. However, judges have been increasingly reluctant to draw a hard-and-fast distinction between 'employee' and 'office holder' and—as demonstrated by *Autoclenz* and *Aslam & Ors*—are much readier than before to look at the factual situation underlying the ostensible terms of engagement. The longer-term effects of *Preston* on how the courts perceive the relationship between ministers of religion and their denominations still remain to be seen—though the recent judgments in *Sharpe*, *Celestial Church of Christ* and *Rev T Harii* are consistent with the Supreme Court's line in *Preston* and it has been given external support by the ECtHR Grand Chamber's decision in *Károly Nagy*.

That said, however, the existing complexities are not difficult to demonstrate. As we have seen, in *Preston* the Court of Appeal held unanimously that Mrs Preston was employed by the Methodist Conference, while the Supreme Court held by four to one that she was not. Lady Hale JSC said in her dissent that

> the relationship between a minister of religion and her Church, which is a temporal one, is not to be confused with the relationship between a minister of religion and her God, which is a spiritual one ... there is nothing intrinsic to religious ministry which is inconsistent with there being a contract between the minister and the Church [36].

She believed, in short, that:

> Everything about this arrangement looks contractual, as did everything about the relationship in the *Percy* case. It was a very specific arrangement for a particular post, at a particular time, with a particular manse and a particular stipend, and with a particular set of responsibilities [49].

So, in the end, four very senior judges took one view while another four very senior judges took the opposite one—but, of course, the Supreme Court trumps the Court of Appeal.

But even if Lady Hale was wrong—and we must assume that she *was* wrong, because her four colleagues disagreed with her—what will happen when, one day in the future, a parish minister in Scotland gets across his or her presbytery, is suspended from ministry by the Judicial Commission of Assembly and ends up in the Court of Session arguing discrimination on the grounds that associate and assistant ministers are given enforceable contracts of employment on appointment but parish ministers are not?[163] The Church might possibly be successful in a plea that the case in question relates to a 'matter spiritual' and is therefore within its exclusive cognisance under the terms of the Church of Scotland Act 1921 and therefore unreviewable—but, there again, it might not. What will *not* save it is the absence of a public law element from the facts of the case, because there no such general requirement in Scots law in order to make the decision of a private tribunal reviewable.[164] As in *Brentnall*, so long as there is a patrimonial interest involved, the Scottish courts are prepared to review the actings of private tribunals—and I would suggest that the outcome of such a case is unpredictable.

Moreover, it is not clear that a public law element would necessarily be required any longer even in England and Wales. In *Otuo*,[165] the claimant had raised an action for slander in respect of words alleged to have been spoken at a meeting at which he was seeking review of his expulsion from the Jehovah's Witnesses. He subsequently sought permission to add a claim for breach of contract in respect of the process leading up to that expulsion and, in dismissing his application, Sir David Eady, sitting as a judge of the High Court, observed:

> I do not believe it can be said, in general terms, that purely because the context of personal relations is religious, therefore there can be no intention to create binding and enforceable legal relations. It must depend on the particular circumstances. *If a body takes upon itself the right to summon people before it, for the purpose of determining such issues as breaches of rules or obligations, and assumes the right to exercise powers of punishment or expulsion, it does not seem to me to be self-evident that such disputes must inevitably fall outside the jurisdiction of the courts.* As with clubs or other associations of members, it may well be possible to infer in some circumstances that there are mutual obligations (e.g. in relation to considerations of natural justice) which the courts could rule upon, and

---

163 A parish minister (as opposed to an associate or an assistant) is still elected and called to his or her pastoral charge by the congregation and continues to be regarded as an office holder for the purposes of employment law. For the procedure for electing and calling a parish minister, see Act VIII 2003 (Vacancy Procedure).

164 For which see *West v Secretary of State for Scotland* 1992 SC 385 (IH).

165 *Otuo v Morley & Anor* [2016] EWHC 46 (QB).

> in respect of which could give certain limited remedies, such as by way of declaration. [7: emphasis added][166]

The Wider Issue of Justiciability

Sir David Eady's conclusion in *Otuo* seems to be some distance from the assertion in *ex parte Wachmann*[167] that the court was not equipped to regulate the determination of whether or not someone was morally and religiously fit to carry out the spiritual and pastoral duties of his office because that determination was essentially a religious function.[168] More generally, it touches on the wider issue of the justiciability of religious disputes.

When issue came before the Supreme Court in *Shergill*,[169] the Court came to the following conclusions:

- 'The law treats unincorporated religious communities as voluntary associations. It views the constitution of a voluntary religious association as a civil contract as it does the contract of association of a secular body: the contract by which members agree to be bound on joining an association sets out the rights and duties of both the members and its governing organs' [46].
- 'The courts will not adjudicate on the decisions of an association's governing bodies unless there is a question of infringement of a civil right or interest. An obvious example of such a civil interest is the loss of a remunerated office. But disputes about doctrine or liturgy are non-justiciable if they do not as a consequence engage civil rights or interests or reviewable questions of public law' [46].
- 'The governing bodies of a religious voluntary association obtain their powers over its members by contract. They must act within the powers conferred by the association's contractual constitution' [47].
- 'Members of a religious association who are dismissed or otherwise subjected to disciplinary procedure may invoke the jurisdiction of the civil courts if the association acts *ultra vires* or breaches in a fundamental way the rules of fair procedure. The jurisdiction of the courts is not excluded because the

166 Coincidentally, the Court of Appeal of Alberta came to a similar conclusion in *Wall v Judicial Committee of the Highwood Congregation of Jehovah's Witnesses* 2016 ABCA 255 (CanLII), which was also about expulsion from the Witnesses—though there was a trenchant dissent by Wakeling JA. It has been appealed to the Supreme Court.

167 *R v Chief Rabbi of the United Hebrew Congregations of Great Britain and the Commonwealth ex parte Wachmann* [1992] 1 WLR 1036.

168 *Per* Simon Brown J at 1042H.

169 *Shergill & Ors v Khaira & Ors* [2014] UKSC 33.

> cause of the disciplinary procedure is a dispute about theology or ecclesiology. The civil court does not resolve the religious dispute. Nor does it decide the merits of disciplinary action if that action is within the contractual powers of the relevant organ of the association ... Its role is more modest: *it keeps the parties to their contract* [48: emphasis added].

In short, the courts will still not adjudicate on the truths of religious beliefs or the validity of particular religious rites in a general sense. But *Shergill* makes it clear that if private rights and obligations depend on religious issues, the court may have to adjudicate on those religious matters that are capable of objective assessment. Doctrinal or liturgical disputes that do not engage private rights or interests or reviewable questions of public law are non-justiciable—but once they begin to do so, they come within the supervisory jurisdiction of the courts.[170]

Ministry, Lay and Ordained

The distinction between an ordained minister and a lay minister might be a very convenient rule of thumb for civil servants, but is it any longer an adequate description of the way in which Churches—and ministry—now operate? In rural areas of England and Scotland, the days of the single parish with a single freehold incumbent or parish minister are pretty well gone for good, while almost all of the Free Churches—certainly in England and Wales—have regarded ministry as a cooperative exercise shared between clergy and laity. Clergy in the Church of England may be stipendiary or 'house-for-duty' and there are at least a few stipendiary (lay) readers. For Methodists, the ministry of lay preachers has always been an essential part of the 'circuit plan', while it is not uncommon for a Baptist congregation to be in the pastoral charge of a stipendiary or house-for-duty lay pastor rather than an ordained minister.

Sandberg (2015) draws attention to Arden LJ's statement in *Sharpe, obiter*, that

170 At the time of writing, the issue of the GOR was before the ECJ in *Vera Egenberger v Evangelisches Werk für Diakonie und Entwicklung e.V.* [2017] EUECJ C-414/16. In his Opinion, Advocate General Tanchev rejected the defendant's submission that the prohibition on State authorities probing the legitimacy of religious beliefs or interfering with the internal organisation of religious bodies excluded the courts from deciding whether a GOR was genuine, legitimate, and justified under Article 4(2) of Directive 2000/78, The ethos of a religion was 'subjective, and quite separate and distinct from the activities entailed in sustaining it, *the latter being an objective matter to be reviewed by courts*' [110: emphasis added].

> [i]n a situation where the shadows of history and tradition are as long as they are here, the court has to be sure that the form does not obscure the present day substance. But, as *Preston* shows, the need to look at the realities cannot require one to disregard the legal arrangements and what they objectively convey.[171]

He suggests that Arden LJ's 'shadows of history and tradition'

> have meant that the employment status of ministers of religion has been seen as a special topic in employment law texts and as a topic worthy of study by law and religion academics. The logical conclusion of the emphasis on the facts as found in the recent cases would seem to question this: separate treatment of this topic seems odd if 'there is now no rule which applies only to ministers'.[172] Yet, the distinctive nature of the facts in disputes concerning clerics would seem to indicate that we have not reached that point yet.

If there is indeed such a rule, it seems to be this: that, in determining the employment status of ministers of religion, the courts will look at the ecclesiology and rules of the Church in question in relation to the status of its clergy. And if the recent cases do nothing else, they demonstrate that the whole issue is still in a state of transition. As Barry Forde points out in the Irish context, on both sides of the border (2017: 93):

> A range of … appointments has emerged in recent years, including Part-Time Stipendiary Ministry with Regulations adopted by the Representative Church Body covering hours of work and providing a model 'Contract *for* Services', yet simply labelling something as other than a contract of employment does not mean that no contract will be implied.[173]

The result—certainly in matters of religion but also more generally—is that the more one looks critically at the murky world of employment law, the less realistic the distinctions between 'workers', 'employees' and 'office holders' seem to appear. Whatever the legal or historical reasons for those distinctions, in terms of current employment policy and practicalities they often seem artificial in the extreme. The categories might have meant something in 1950—and

171 *Sharpe v Bishop of Worcester* [2015] EWCA Civ 399 [108].

172 *Sharpe v Bishop of Worcester* [2015] EWCA Civ 399 [60].

173 [emphasis in original].

might even have been found to be helpful—but is that still the case in a world of interns, zero-hours contracts, agency workers, individual contractors, consultants and the National Minimum/Living Wage?

A Suitable Case for Reform?

In July 2017, the report of an independent review of modern working practices commissioned by the Prime Minister and chaired by Matthew Taylor, former Chief Adviser on Strategy to Tony Blair when he was Prime Minister and currently Chief Executive of the Royal Society of Arts, had this to say about the current state of the law:

> Regardless of how they are employed, whether in a traditional, full-time role or on a more flexible basis, people should understand what rights they have. Even many individuals working in the most casual of relationships are entitled to basic employment rights and should be aware of this. Employment status is the gateway through which an individual must go to access statutory rights. As we have said, determining employment status must be simpler, clearer, and give individuals and employers more information, a greater level of certainty and an understanding of which rights and responsibilities apply.
>
> We feel it is time that Government takes a fresh look at the legislation. Clearer legislation should improve the ability of citizens, and those who support them, to understand what employment status applies and what rights they are entitled to. While better guidance plays its part, legislation that reflects the reality of the modern workplace is a key driver and must be the starting point ...
>
> More clearly and definitively stating the basis for employment status in legislation will not be easy. However, as a number of organisations ... recognise, there is now an overwhelming case to tackle this sooner rather than later.
>
> *Government should replace the minimalistic approach to legislation with a clearer outline of the tests for employment status, setting out the key principles in primary legislation, and using secondary legislation and guidance to provide more detail.* (2017: 35: authors' emphasis).

Though the review was set up primarily to look at the legal implications of the so-called 'gig economy' and makes no reference whatsoever to the employment status of office holders, it ranges far more widely than zero-hours contracts, suggesting that 'Ultimately, if it looks and feels like employment, it should have the status and protection of employment' (2017: 36). But that begs the question, 'So how do you know whether it *does* look and feel like employment?' The relationship in the *Preston/Moore* litigation looked and felt like employment to the Court of Appeal—but not to a majority of the Supreme Court.

Whether anything will come of the Taylor Review's recommendations, only time will tell; but my final thoughts are these. Employment practices have changed out of all recognition in the last fifty years, so do any of the current distinctions still serve a useful purpose? And might the question of employment status generally—not just employment in religious organisations—be a suitable subject for future consideration by the three Law Commissions?

List of References

Advisory Conciliation and Arbitration Service. 2014. *Religion or belief and the workplace*. ACAS, London. <http://www.acas.org.uk/media/pdf/d/n/Religion-or-Belief-and-the_workplace-guide.pdf>.

Alidadi K. 2017. *Religion, Equality and Employment in Europe: The Case for Reasonable Accommodation*: Hart Publishing, Oxford and Portland, Oregon.

Anon. 2017. '*Hickey v McGowan*: Member of religious order held vicariously liable for sexual abuse by another member' SCOIRBLOG, 12 February. <https://scoirl.wordpress.com/2017/02/12/hickey-v-mcgowan-member-of-religious-order-held-vicariously-liable-for-sexual-abuse-by-another-member/>.

Brown C.G., Green G. and Mair J. 2016. *Religion in Scots Law: The Report of an Audit at the University of Glasgow*. Humanist Society Scotland, Edinburgh. <https://www.humanism.scot/wp-content/uploads/2016/02/Religion-in-Scots-Law-Final-Report-22-Feb-16.pdf>.

Church of England. 2014. *The Deployment of Clergy with licences and permission to officiate* (PTO). Archbishops' Council, London. <https://www.churchofengland.org/media/4004867/deployment-of-clergy-with-licences-and-pto-june-2014.pdf>.

Church of England. 2016. *Canons of the Church of England*, 7th edition. General Synod, London. <https://www.churchofengland.org/about-us/structure/churchlawlegis/canons/canons-7th-edition.aspx>.

Church of England. 2017a. General Synod. *Archbishops' Guidelines on the Implementation of "Choosing Bishops"—The Equality Act 2010 (Revised)* (GS Misc 1044). General Synod, London. <https://www.churchofengland.org/media/4009893/AB-Guidelines-on-GS-Misc-1044-July-2017.pdf>.

Church of England. 2017b. General Synod Legal Advisory Commission. *The Parish Music: organists and choirmasters and church musicians*. Archbishops' Council, London. <https://www.churchofengland.org/media/3956676/organists.pdf>

Cranmer F. 2011. '*Maga* and Vicarious Liability for Sexual Abuse', 167 *Law & Justice* 20.

Cranmer F. 2014. 'Marriage, Roman Catholic clergy and Article 8 ECHR: *Fernández Martínez v Spain*' *Law & Religion UK*, 16 June. <http://www.lawandreligionuk.com/2014/06/16/marriage-roman-catholic-clergy-and-article-8-echr-fernandez-martinez-v-spain/>.

Cranmer F. 2015. 'Wales and the Law of Marriage: "Vestiges of Establishment" Revisited', 174 *Law & Justice* 96.

Cranmer F. 2017. 'Strasbourg upholds Belgian *niqab* ban: *Belcacemi* and *Dakir*', *Law & Religion UK*, 12 July. <http://www.lawandreligionuk.com/2017/07/12/strasbourg-upholds-belgian-niqab-ban-belcacemi-and-dakir/>.

Cranmer F. and Peterson S. 2006. 'Employment, Sex Discrimination and the Churches: The Percy Case', 8 *Ecclesiastical Law Journal* 392.

Doe N. 1996. *The Legal Framework of the Church of England*: Clarendon Press, Oxford.

Doe N. 1998. *Canon Law in the Anglican Communion*. Clarendon Press, Oxford.

Equality and Human Rights Commission. 2016. *Religion or belief—is the law working?* EHRC, London. <https://www.equalityhumanrights.com/sites/default/files/religion-or-belief-report-december-2016.pdf>.

Forde B. 2017. 'Church of Ireland clergy and employment law' 178 *Law & Justice* 81–100.

Free Church of Scotland. 2014. *Free Church Practice*. Free Church of Scotland, Edinburgh. <https://freechurch.org/resources/free-church-practice>.

Gainsbury S. 2010. 'Fresh guidance on "bare below the elbow"', *Nursing Times*, 30 March.

Gibson M. 2013. 'The God "Dilution"? Religion, Discrimination and the Case for Reasonable Accommodation', 72(3) *Cambridge Law Journal* 578.

Gillen P. and Morgan B. 2013. *Comparative analysis of employment law in Great Britain, Northern Ireland and the Republic of Ireland*. CBI Northern Ireland, Belfast. <http://www.pinsentmasons.com/ELP/CBI%20-%20Comparative%20Analysis%20of%20Employment%20Law.pdf>.

Hale B. M [Baroness Hale of Richmond]. 2014a. 'Religion and Sexual Orientation: The clash of equality rights', lecture at the Comparative and Administrative Law Conference, Yale Law School. 7 March. <https://www.supremecourt.uk/docs/speech-140307.pdf>.

Hale B. M [Baroness Hale of Richmond]. 2014b. 'Freedom of Religion and Belief', Annual Human Rights Lecture for the Law Society of Ireland. 13 June. <https://www.supremecourt.uk/docs/speech-140613.pdf>.

Hall H. 2011. '*Maga* and Direct Liability in Negligence', 167 *Law & Justice* 11.

Handley K.R. 2011. 'Sham self-employment', 127 *Law Quarterly Review* 171.

Hill M. 2007. *Ecclesiastical Law*. Oxford University Press, Oxford.

Hill M. 2013. 'Religion at work', 163 *New Law Journal* 1 February.

Hopper T. 2014. 'Teen felt "degraded" after teacher backed aikido student's request to avoid touching females on religious grounds', *National Post* 14 January.

Howard E. 2013. 'Reasonable Accommodation of Religion and Other Discrimination Grounds in EU Law', 38 *European Law Review* 360.

HM Government. nd. *Employing People: contracts of employment and working hours: employment status*. <https://www.gov.uk/employment-status>.

HM Revenue & Customs. 2016. *PAYE70230—PAYE operation: specific employments: clergy and ministers of religion*. London. <https://www.gov.uk/hmrc-internal-manuals/paye-manual/paye70230#IDA31SIH>.

Jennings P. 2013. 'Tribunal watch: religion or belief discrimination', *Bates Wells & Braithwaite Employment Law Update—Early Spring* 12. <http://www.bwbllp.com/file/employment-update-spring-2013-linked-pdf>.

Lyall F. 2016. *Church and State in Scotland: Developing Law*. Routledge, London & New York.

McLynn L. and Cook V. 2016. 'Volunteer status—they think it's all over ... but it isn't', *Bates Wells & Braithwaite Charity and Social Enterprise Update—Autumn* 16. <http://i.emlfiles1.com/cmpdoc/9/4/0/1/9/files/399642_bwb-autumn-charity-update-2016.pdf?utm_source=Bates%20Wells%20Braithwaite&utm_medium=email&utm_campaign=7587111_Charity%20Update%20Autumn%202016&dm_i=1Y95,4IM93,EQ22GV,GPOI9,1>.

Montini G. [Pope Paul VI]. 1965. *Pastoral Constitution on the Church in the Modern World, Gaudium et Spes, promulgated by His Holiness, Pope Paul VI on December 7, 1965*. The Vatican <http://www.vatican.va/archive/hist_councils/ii_vatican_council/documents/vat-ii_const_19651207_gaudium-et-spes_en.html>.

Moore E.G. 1992. *Moore's Introduction to English Canon Law*. Mowbray. London [3rd *edn*, Briden T. and Hanson B. *eds*].

NatCen. 2017. 'Religious affiliation among adults in Great Britain', *British Social Attitudes Survey 34*. <http://www.bsa.natcen.ac.uk/media/39203/bsa-religion.pdf>.

Office for National Statistics (ONS): *2011 Census, Key Statistics for Local Authorities in England and Wales*.

Office for National Statistics (ONS): 2014. *A closer look at the answers to the "What is your religion?" question on the 2011 Census*. <http://webarchive.nationalarchives.gov.uk/20160105160709/http://www.ons.gov.uk/ons/rel/census/2011-census/key-statistics-for-local-authorities-in-england-and-wales/sty-what-is-your-religion.html>.

Office for National Statistics (ONS): 2016. *Population estimates*. <http://www.ons.gov.uk/peoplepopulationandcommunity/populationandmigration/populationestimates>.

Percy H. 2011. *Scandalous, Immoral and Improper—The Trial of Helen Percy*. Argyll Publishing, Glendaruel.

Pyper D. 2015. *The National Minimum Wage: volunteers and interns*. Library Briefing Paper Number 00697. House of Commons, London.

Sandberg R. 2014. *Religion, Law and Society*. Cambridge UP. Cambridge.

Sandberg R. 2015. 'Not a Sharpe Turn: a note on *Sharpe v Bishop of Worcester*', *Law & Religion UK*, 2 May. <http://www.lawandreligionuk.com/2015/05/02/not-a-sharpe-turn-a-note-on-sharpe-v-bishop-of-worcester/>.

Shaw C.J.D. [Lord Kilbrandon] *et al.* 1964, republished 2003. *Children and Young Persons Scotland: Report by the Committee Appointed by the Secretary of State for Scotland.* HMSO, Edinburgh.

Strauss M. 2016. 'Dismissal in schools with a religious character—Human Rights and Equality Law', Farrer & Co *WorkLife*, 14 October. <http://www.farrer.co.uk/how-we-help/employment-issues/WorkLife/WorkLife/Dates/2016/10/Dismissal-in-schools-with-a-religious-character---Human-Rights-and-Equality-Law-/>.

Taylor M. 2017. '*Good Work: The Taylor Review of Modern Working Practices*'. HM Government, London.

Unite the Union. 2107. 'Faith Workers Branch'. <http://www.unitefaithworkers.org.uk>.

Vickers L. 2009. 'Religion and Belief Discrimination and the Employment of Teachers in Faith Schools', 4 *Religion and Human Rights* 1.

Vickers L. 2010. 'Religious Discrimination in the Workplace: An Emerging Hierarchy?', 12 *Ecclesiastical Law Journal* 280.

Vickers L. 2014. 'Conform or be confined: *S.A.S. v France*', *Oxford Human Rights Hub Blog*. <http://humanrights.dev3.oneltd.eu/?p=12011>.

Vickers L. 2015. 'Law, religion and the workplace', in Ferrari S. ed. *Routledge Handbook of Law and Religion*. Routledge, London & New York.

Vickers L. 2016. *Religious Freedom, Religious Discrimination and the Workplace*. Hart Publishing, Oxford 2nd edition.

Watkin T.G. 1990. 'Vestiges of Establishment: The Ecclesiastical and Canon Law of the Church in Wales', 7 *Ecclesiastical Law Journal* 110.

Wren A. 2017. 'Headscarves in the workplace a thing of the past?! Well, not surprisingly, no …', Farrer & Co *WorkLife*, 17 March <http://www.farrer.co.uk/how-we-help/employment-issues/WorkLife/WorkLife/Dates/2017/3/Headscarves-in-the-workplace-a-thing-of-the-past--Well-not-surprisingly-no/?utm_source=vuture&utm_medium=email&utm_campaign=worklife%20subscribers%20weekly_17%20march%202017>.

Table of Cases

A v Watchtower Bible and Tract Society (Trustees of) & Ors [2015] EWHC 1722 (QB).

Ahtinen v Finland [2008] ECHR 882.

Aslam & Ors v Uber BV & Ors [2016] UKET 2202500/2015.

Asma Bougnaoui and l'Association de défense des droits de l'homme (ADDH) *v Micropole SA* [2016] EUECJ C188/15.

Autoclenz Ltd v Belcher & Ors [2011] UKSC 41.

Barthorpe v Exeter Diocesan Board of Finance [1979] ICR 900.

Begum v Pedagogy Auras UK Ltd (t/a Barley Lane Montessori Day Nursery) [2015] UKEAT 0309/13/2205.

Belcacemi and Oussar v Belgium [2017] ECHR 655.

Bougnaoui and ADDH [2017] EUECJ C-188/15.

Brentnall v Free Presbyterian Church of Scotland 1986 SLT 471.

Buckley v Cahal Daly [1990] NIJB 8.

Bull & Anor v Hall & Anor [2013] UKSC 73.

Campbell and Cosans v United Kingdom [1982] ECHR 1.

Catholic Child Welfare Society & Ors v Various Claimants and The Institute of the Brothers of the Christian Schools [2012] UKSC 56.

Celestial Church of Christ, Edward Street Parish (A Charity) v Lawson [2017] EWHC 97 (Ch).

Chandra v Arya Samaj Vedic Mission (West Midlands) [2014] Birmingham County Court (unreported).

Chatwal v Wandsworth Borough Council (Religion or Belief Discrimination) [2011] UKEAT 0487/10/0607.

Cherfi v G4S Security Services Ltd [2011] UKEAT 0379/10/2405.

Copsey v WBB Devon Clays Ltd [2005] EWCA Civ 932.

Cox v Ministry of Justice [2016] UKSC 10.

Dakir v Belgium [2017] ECHR 656.

Davies v Presbyterian Church of Wales [1986] ICR 280.

Diocese of Southwark v Coker [1998] ICR 140.

Doe v Bennett & Ors 2004 SCC 17.

Drew v Walsall Healthcare NHS Trust [2013] UKEAT 0378/12/2009.

Dudová and Duda v Czech Republic [2001] ECHR No. 40224/98

Ebrahimian v France [2015] ECHR 1041.

Essop & Ors v Home Office (UK Border Agency) [2017] UKSC 27.

Eweida and Others v United Kingdom [2013] ECHR 37.

F and S v TH [2016] EWHC 1605 (QB).

Fernández Martínez v Spain [2014] ECHR 615.

Fhima v Travel Jigsaw Ltd [2015] UKET (unreported).

Forbes v Eden (1865) 4 M 143: [1867] 1HL Sc and Div 568.

G v P [2013] Ashford Employment Tribunal (unreported).

G v St Gregory's Catholic Science College [2011] EWHC 1452 (Admin).

G4S Secure Solutions NV [2017] EUECJ C-157/15.

Ganga v Chelmsford Diocesan Board of Finance and the Bishop of Chelmsford in corporate capacity [2015] UKET 3200933/2013.

Gareddu v London Underground Ltd [2016] UKEAT 0086/16/1512.

General Assembly of the Free Church of Scotland v Lord Overtoun: Macalister v Young [1904] AC 515, 1904 7 F (HL) 1.
Glasgow City Council v McNab [2007] UKEAT 0037/06/1701.
Grainger Plc & Ors v Nicholson [2009] UKEAT 0219/09/0311.
Halawi v WDFG UK Ltd (t/a World Duty Free) [2014] EWCA Civ 1387.
Hanna and Peter Müller v Germany [2008] ECHR 12986/04.
Harris v NKL Automotive Ltd & Anor [2007] UKEAT 0134/07/0310.
Hender v Prospects for People with Learning Disabilities [2008] UKET 2902090/2006.
Hickey v McGowan & Ors [2017] IESC 6.
Holland v Angel Supermarket Ltd & Anor [2013] UKET 3301005/2013.
Hudson v TPG Web Publishing Ltd & Ors [2011] UKET 2200565/11.
In re National Insurance Act 1911, On Employment of Church of England Curates [1912] 2 Ch 563.
Islington v Ladele [2008] UKEAT 0453/08/1912.
JGE v English Province of Our Lady of Charity & Anor [2011] EWHC 2871 (QB).
JGE v Portsmouth Roman Catholic Diocesan Trust [2012] EWCA Civ 938.
Kalaç v Turkey [1997] ECHR 37.
Károly Nagy v Hungary [2015] ECHR 1051: [2017] ECHR 782.
Lee v Chung and Shun Shing Construction & Engineering Co Ltd [1990] IRLR 236.
Macdonald v Free Presbyterian Church of Scotland [2010] UKEAT 0034/09/1002.
Macdonald, Re Application for Judicial Review [2010] ScotCS CSOH 55.
Maga v Trustees of the Birmingham Archdiocese of the Roman Catholic Church [2010] EWCA Civ 256.
Majrowski v Guy's and St Thomas' NHS Trust [2006] UKHL 34.
Mba v London Borough of Merton [2012] UKEAT 0332/12/1312: [2013] EWCA Civ 1562.
Mbuyi v Newpark Childcare (Shepherds Bush) Ltd [2015] UKET 3300656/2014.
Miller v Secretary of State for Home Affairs [2004] UKEAT 00926/03/0405.
Miss M Keens-Betts v The Anthony Gregg Partnership Ltd [2017] UKET 2208102/2016.
Mohamud v WM Morrison Supermarkets plc [2016] UKSC 11.
Moore v President of the Methodist Conference [2010] UKEAT 0219/10/1503.
Mr R Kiss v Dephna Estates Ltd and others [2017] UKET 2205945/2016.
Mrs S Kuteh v Dartford and Gravesham NHS Trust [2017] UKET 2302764/2016.
Muhammed v Leprosy Mission International [2009] UKET 2303459/09.
New Testament Church of God v Stewart [2007] EWCA Civ 1004.
Obst v Germany [2010] ECHR No. 425/03.
Ontario Human Rights Commission (O'Malley) v Simpsons-Sears 1985 CanLII 18 (SCC).
Otuo v Morley & Anor [2016] EWHC 46 (QB).
Pemberton v Inwood, Acting Bishop of Southwell and Nottingham [2015] UKET 2600962/2014.
Pemberton v Inwood [2016] UKEAT 0072/16/0712.

Percy v Board of National Mission of the Church [2001] ScotCS CSIH 65.

Percy v Church of Scotland Board of National Mission [2005] UKHL 73.

Piper v Maidstone & Tunbridge Wells NHS Trust [2012] UKEAT 0359/12/1812.

President of the Methodist Conference v Parfitt [1984] ICR 176.

President of the Methodist Conference v Preston [2011] EWCA Civ 1581: [2013] UKSC 29.

R v Chief Rabbi of the United Hebrew Congregations of Great Britain and the Commonwealth ex parte Wachmann [1992] 1 WLR 1036.*R (Amicus MSF Section) v Secretary of State for Trade and Industry* [2004] EWHC 860.

R (Brown) v Canal River Trust [2012] EWHC 3133 (Admin).

R (UNISON) v Lord Chancellor [2017] UKSC 51.

Raggett v Society of Jesus Trust of 1929 for Roman Catholic Purposes & Anor [2010] EWCA Civ 1002.

Rahman v Ministry of Justice [2017] UKET 2300311/2016.

Ready Mixed Concrete (South East) Limited v Minister of Pensions & National Insurance [1968] 1 AER 433.

Reaney v Hereford Diocesan Board of Finance [2007] UKET 1602844/2006.

Rev T Harii v Tasso Baptist Church and London Baptist Association [2017] UKET 2206435/2016.

S.A.S. v France [2014] ECHR 695.

Samira Achbita & Anor v G4S Secure Solutions NV [2016] EUECJ C-157/15.

Schüth v Germany [2010] ECHR No. 1620/03.

Sharpe v Bishop of Worcester [2015] EWCA Civ 399.

Sharpe v Worcester Diocesan Board and the Bishop of Worcester [2012] UKET 1302291/2008.

Sharpe v Worcester Diocesan Board of Finance Ltd & Anor [2013] UKEAT 0243/12/2811.

Shergill & Ors v Khaira & Ors [2014] UKSC 33.

Sheridan v Prospects for People with Learning Disabilities [2008] UKET 2901366/2006.

Sholl v PCC of St Michael & All Angels w St James, Croydon & Anor [2011] UKET 2330072/2010.

Siebenhaar v Germany [2011] ECHR No. 18136/02.

Sindicatul Păstorul Cel Bun v Romania [2012] ECHR No. 2330/09: [2013] ECHR 646.

Singh v Management Committee of the Bristol Sikh Temple & Ors [2012] UKEAT 0429/11/1402.

Travaš v Croatia [2016] ECHR 813.

Trayhorn v Secretary of State for Justice [2017] UKEAT 0304/16/0108.

Various Claimants v The Catholic Child Welfare Society and the Institute of Brothers of the Christian Schools & Ors [2010] EWCA Civ 1106.

Vento v Chief Constable of West Yorkshire Police [2002] EWCA Civ 1871.

Vera Egenberger v Evangelisches Werk für Diakonie und Entwicklung e.V. [2017] EUECJ C-414/16.
Vetta v London Dreams Motion Pictures Ltd [2010] UKET 2703377/08.
Wall v Judicial Committee of the Highwood Congregation of Jehovah's Witnesses 2016 ABCA 255 (CanLII).
Wasteney v East London NHS Foundation Trust [2015] UKET 3200658/2014: [2016] UKEAT 0157/15/0704.
West v Secretary of State for Scotland 1992 SC 385 (IH).
X v Mid Sussex Citizens Advice Bureau & Anor [2012] UKSC 59.

Table of Legislation

Act III 2001 (Discipline of Ministry) [Church of Scotland].
Act VIII 2003 (Vacancy Procedure) [Church of Scotland].
Church Act 1990 [Hungary].
Church Act 1993 [Finland].
Clergy Discipline Measure 2003.
Constitution Act 1982 [Canada].
Council Directive 93/104/EC of 23 November 1993 concerning certain aspects of the organization of working time.
Council Directive 2000/78/EC of 27 November 2000 establishing a general framework for equal treatment in employment and occupation.
Disability Discrimination Act 1995.
Ecclesiastical Offices (Terms of Service) Regulations 2009.
Ecclesiastical Offices (Terms of Service) Measure 2009.
Ecclesiastical Offices (Terms of Service) Directions 2010.
Employment Equality (Religion or Belief) Regulations 2003.
Employment Equality (Sexual Orientation) Regulations 2003.
Employment Rights Act 1996.
Employment Rights (Northern Ireland) Order 1996.
Employment Tribunals and the Employment Appeal Tribunal Fees Order 2013.
Equality Act 2010.
Extra-Parochial Ministry Measure 1967.
Fair Employment and Treatment (Northern Ireland) Order 1998.
Irish Church Act 1869.
Limitation Act 1980.
National Minimum Wage Act 1998.
National Minimum Wage Regulations 1999.

National Minimum Wage Regulations 2015.
Prison Act 1952.
Protection from Harassment Act 1997.
Scotland Act 1998.
Sex Discrimination Act 1975.
Government of Wales Act 1998.
Government of Wales Act 2006.
Wales Act 2017.
Welsh Church Act 1914.
Working Time Regulations 1998.